YORKSHIRE VILLAINS

ROGUES, RASCALS AND REPROBATES

Contents

Acknowledgements

My sincere thanks go to the team at The History Press, who have encouraged me and offered advice throughout the process of writing this book. My special thanks go to Beth Amphlett, who suggested the book to me as one I might be interested in. As always, my gratitude goes to the staff at the Sheffield Library and Archives Service and the Rotherham Archives and Local Studies Department. I always tell them that it would be impossible to do my job without them. During the research for this book I was helped enormously by the staff at the Explore York Library, who were unfailingly helpful. Permission was granted for the use of photographs of the Gaoler's and Chaplain's respective journals, and the Calendar of Felons were from the originals held at the City of York Council Archives and Local History department. My very grateful thanks go to the staff at York Castle Prison Museum, who were also extremely obliging. Permission for the reproduction of the photographs of the castle and its surroundings was given by the York Museum Trust. I am particularly grateful for the research undertaken by Jackie Logan of the York Museums Trust regarding the position of the original gallows, and for the photograph of the site by Richard Stansfield also from the York Museum Trust. The photographs of the area in and around Halifax were taken by my niece Sue Trickey, to whom I would like to dedicate this book

Thank you to everyone for their help!

Introduction

As an author, I have been fortunate enough to be able to write about the things I enjoy most, and, when two areas of interest combine, it is arguably much more pleasurable. When writing *Yorkshire Villains: Rogues, Rascals and Reprobates*, I knew I could combine two of my passions – true crime and Yorkshire. I have always considered myself to be a Yorkshire girl at heart, having been brought up amongst those dark, satanic mills of Halifax, West Yorkshire. Most of my life has been spent based around Huddersfield, Bradford, Sowerby Bridge and Leeds, so I know the areas and the people well. Yorkshire, evidently named after the city of York (or Yorvik to give its ancient Viking name), is one of the largest counties in Britain. To me, the county encapsulates the range of the different landscapes of Britain; from the rugged beauty of the North Yorkshire Dales, to the heavily industrialised cities of West and South Yorkshire. The East Yorkshire area contains within it the stunning coastline and the ancient towns of Hull and Beverley. The period of this book ranges from 1800–1900. During this period of time, the county was divided into three 'Ridings', also named by the Vikings, which translates literally as 'a third part'. There was much opposition in 1974 when the ancient Viking name was lost, and the county was separated into South, North, East and West Yorkshire. However, for the purpose of continuity I have specified which part of Yorkshire the cases take place (i.e. NR= North Riding). I have also included places which are now no longer in Yorkshire (i.e. Middlesborough), for the reason that during the nineteenth century they all formed part of the same county.

Crime in Yorkshire was usually undertaken out of sheer necessity; within this book, however, the villains who plotted and

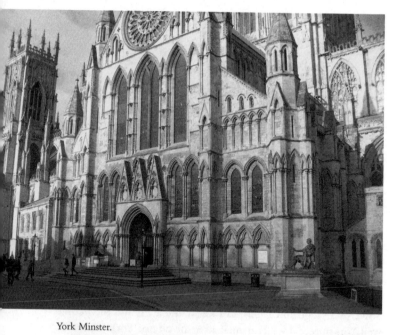

York Minster.

Queen Victoria statue, Hull.

The only remaining section left of St Mary's churchyard, Castlegate.

carried out their crimes with cold, calculated brutality and violence take centre stage. Traditionally, prisoners would be tried at the local magistrates' courts, and, if found guilty, they would then have to be tried at the York Assizes. Sentencing for these more serious crimes could be a term of imprisonment, transportation or the death sentence. Some who received the death sentence were buried in St Mary's churchyard in Castlegate, York, although much of the area is now built on and only a small part of the churchyard remains. The less fortunate were sentenced to be hanged, their bodies later being sent for dissection. The York Assizes were held at the York Castle, but prisoners from all over Yorkshire were punished at the gallows there. One of the earliest recorded executions was a man known as Roger de Clifford, who was hanged at the tower that would later be named after him in 1322. Many of the executions were public hangings where there was often a carnival-like atmosphere in the crowd. At first, all the Assizes for Yorkshire were held at York and the expenses shared by the police authorities of the three Ridings. But by June 1864, the level of crime for the West Riding area was so high that it was agreed that a separate assizes court would be held at Leeds. Hangings at Leeds were undertaken at Armley Gaol, although

The original castle keep, now known as Clifford's Tower. (Courtesy of York Museum Trust)

there was only one public hanging before the decision was made that the rest would be completed in private. Nevertheless, spectators would still gather outside the prison gates to be there when the criminals were executed.

I use the term 'villains' of Yorkshire somewhat loosely within this book; some criminals in this book protested their innocence to the end, and, in some cases, were proved right. Many of those who were hung or imprisoned for their crimes saw themselves as 'political prisoners' rather than criminals. Nevertheless, the authorities saw them all as villains and their sentences as just.

Margaret Drinkall, 2011

Chapter One

Highway Robbery

One of the most audacious crimes committed during the nineteenth century was that of highway robbery. Numerous tall tales and romantic legends have sprung up over the years about the highwaymen, as they became known. One of the most famous is that of Dick Turpin, who was hanged at York on 17 April 1789. In reality, their deaths were used as a warning to others, and many of the executed bodies were hanged on gibbets and left to rot, continuing the punishment and humiliation even after death. Another highwayman, one Spence Broughton, who robbed the Rotherham Mail Coach and was hung at York on 14 April 1792, suffered the same fate as Turpin. After being hanged, his body was then relocated to Attercliffe Common, near Sheffield, where the robbery had occurred; he gruesomely hung on a gibbet for thirty-six years. Despite their romantic reputation, highway robbers of this period carried out their exploits with much violence and intimidation.

One such notorious highway robber of Yorkshire was a villain named Joseph Riley, who, like Dick Turpin before him, had a large amount of luck in his escapades. On the night of 23 May 1837, Riley committed not one but two highway robberies. Riley and four other acquaintances met at the Waterloo Bridge at Leeds (WR), waiting in ambush for the book keeper of Messrs S. Davis

The hologram of Dick Turpin, seen in the original condemned cell at York Castle. He made the journey to the gallows. (Courtesy of York Museum Trust)

and Company to arrive. Targeted was a Mr Terry; he did not see the five men approaching him until he was brutally knocked onto the floor. Whilst being held face down by three of the robbers, Riley went through Mr Terry's pockets and extracted a silver watch and chain. Despite the fact that it was a very dark night, Terry recognised Riley and after the robbery he gave his name to the local constable, PC Stubbs. That same night, a farmer from Wortley, near Leeds, was robbed of a knife and handkerchief and 15s in change. The farmer, Mr Sunderland, also recognised Riley, and the next morning the constables went to his father's house to arrest him. On searching the property they found that he had escaped from a hatch leading out of the coal cellar. Following information that a stolen silver watch belonging to Mr Terry had been seen in Riley's possession, a warrant for his arrest was signed by a Justice of the Peace. For a while he lay low, but he was eventually captured when he tried his luck once again at Brotherton, near Pontefract (WR), on the 20 August. An unnamed gentleman, who he had robbed, raised the alarm and Riley took to his heels and ran into some fields. Being unfamiliar with the area, he leapt over a wall bordering a stone quarry which was 36ft deep. The fall failed to kill him, leaving him with a broken leg, and he was taken to the Leeds Infirmary for treatment. The kindly gentleman who he had robbed felt that he had suffered enough, and, when asked by the constable if he wanted to prosecute Riley, he stated that he didn't want to take the case any further. When Riley was tried at Leeds for his repeated offences of highway robbery, there were plenty of witnesses who identified him as one of a gang of robbers. With such overwhelming evidence, the jury had no option but to send him straight for trial at the York Assizes. When Riley came into court on Thursday 27 December in front of the judge, Robert Baynes Armstrong Esq., he was very fortunate to receive a lenient sentence of prison for just three months.

Assizes judges saw themselves as figures of great authority and their arrival in the assizes towns were treated with much pomp and circumstance. Such was their authority that in some cases they even disagreed with the jury's verdict. Howden (ER) in 1839 was a quiet market town dominated by the spire of the Minster, which was built in the eighth century. It might be described as a place where crime was relatively unknown. So it was with some wonder to the inhabitants when on the night of 13 December it was heard that a highway robbery had taken place. The victims, Peter Waterhouse and his wife, had visited a public house that evening to see their friend, the landlord named Jackson, at approximately 8 p.m. Following a merry party, the pair proceeded home on the road which was brightly lit by moonlight. They had almost reached Howden when there suddenly appeared three masked men and Waterhouse saw that one of the men held a pistol. The man with the gun shouted 'deliver' and Waterhouse, thinking he was joking, tried to push past, but the man raised the gun. He angrily repeated, 'Deliver or I will blow your brains out, deliver damn you!' Waterhouse, stunned by what was happening, said that he had nothing of value on his person, but the masked man found a watch which he put in his pocket. After the robbers had absconded, the couple went back to Jackson's public house and told them what had happened. A constable was sent for, and, when PC Auty arrived, he was instructed to search two local lodging houses for any suspicious men. None were found, but the following day a prisoner named James Sheldon (24), was arrested and identified by Waterhouse. Sheldon denied stealing the watch or being in Jackson's establishment that night – stating that he had not been down that particular road since erecting a booth at the fair many months before. Another witness disagreed, saying that Sheldon had been at Jackson's public house but had remained behind until half an hour after the Waterhouses had left. At the Assizes on 9 March 1839, the Judge Baron Alderson outlined the case methodically for the jury – but when they brought in a verdict of guilty, to their great surprise, the judge stated that he did not agree and he thought Sheldon to be innocent. He ordered that Sheldon should be kept in custody until further enquiries were made. The astonishment of the court resulted in much murmuring against the learned judge as he proceeded with the next case, which was again of highway robbery at Almondbury (WR). In this case, too, a watch had been stolen and the robber was apprehended when he tried to pawn it. When the jury found this man guilty, Baron Alderson sentenced him to transportation for life. It was known that judges frowned on the violence used in these kind of cases, and that sentences of transportation were becoming more common.

Halifax (WR) was at the centre of the woollen trade since the fifteenth century. Pride of place in the centre of the town is the historic Piece Hall, where the woollen cloth pieces were bought and sold. Artisans of the woollen trade were becoming quite wealthy in the first half of the nineteenth century, and many could now afford such luxuries as a horse and gig. Such a person was a worsted spinner, Mr Crossley, accompanied by a friend, Mr Thomas Cockroft, who went for a day out to Wakefield (WR) on 6 August 1839. At about 9 p.m., the two men decided to return back to Halifax, and as they approached the town they saw four men on the road walking towards them. When the men saw the gig approaching, they spread out across the road, forcing the horse to stop. One of the men grabbed the horse's bridle and Mr Crossley stood up and lashed out at him with his whip. Crossley's self defence was to no avail, however, and another member of the aggressive gang pulled him out of the gig, throwing him against a wall. His gold watch was stolen along with some money, but, whilst the robbery was in progress, Crossley recognised one of the men as

The historic Piece Hall in Halifax. (Courtesy of Sue Trickey)

The entrance to the Piece Hall, Halifax.

North Bridge, Halifax.

Wilson Barber (21), who he had seen previously on the streets of Halifax. Crossley begged the gang to let him go, saying, 'You may take my money but please spare my life.' The men continued to use very abusive language to both victims, although it was reported that one of the gang tried to restrain his more violent colleagues, urging them to 'let the two men go'.

Meanwhile, upon seeing the men stop the gig, Crossely's companion, Cockroft, was terrified and jumped out of the vehicle, running into a field full of high grass. Barber jumped over the wall into the field and pursued him, followed by two companions, later identified as Michael Dawson (19) and Robert Tittering (22). A fourth man, later identified as Jonathon Rushworth (32), held Crossley to the floor whilst the others pursued Cockroft. They caught him and, whilst rifling through his pockets, found his watch and some money. Once again threatening the men that they would return and kill the pair of them, the four men disappeared into the night. By now, badly shaken, the two men got back into the gig and continued on their way to Halifax where they reported the robbery to the police. A warrant was issued for all the men. Barber and Rushworth were seen at Barnsley Racecourse two days later by the police. Before they could be arrested, they shouted to the congregating crowds that they were

A view of Halifax, taken from Southowram Bank. (Courtesy of Sue Trickey)

Chartists and the police were harassing them. There was much approval for the Chartists at that time and the crowd started to abuse the police, who were eventually forced to let them go. Despite this escape, the two men were later arrested when they returned back to Halifax. Titterington and Dawson had fled to Dublin and, when he was apprehended, it was found that Dawson had a loaded pistol in his pocket. When Tittering was arrested, the police found both stolen watches and a large quantity of bank notes in his possession. Tittering stated that his name was Thompson, and when he was asked why he had the gold watch on his person, he told the arresting officers that he was a travelling jeweller and the watch was his. This was doubted as the name of 'Mr Crossley' was engraved on the watch. The men were all brought to the York Assizes on 14 March 1840 charged with highway robbery, the theft of two watches and ten £5 notes. The two watches were identified by both Crossley and Cockroft as being the same ones that were stolen on the night of the robbery. The jury gave the guilty verdict and the judge sentenced Dawson, Tittering and Barber to transportation for life. Rushworth received a reduced sentence of fifteen years' transportation, as he had urged his colleagues to let the two men go. Transportation was an alternative to prison or hanging for some cases during this period. Convicts were sent out to serve their time in colonies such as Western Australia or Van Diemen's Land (later Tasmania). As transportees, the men would lead lives of hard, back-breaking work on roads and the farms of such colonies, in the heat and dust, no doubt wishing they were back in the coolness of the Yorkshire countryside. The very young ages of these robbers would ensure that they would have spent many years undertaking this punishment many miles from home.

Another case which resulted in the villains being transported for highway robbery took place on New Year's Eve in 1840. A farmer, William Whitehead, living at Barwick in Elmet (WR), went to usher in the New Year with friends at Bradford. No doubt carried away with the alcohol he had consumed, he decided that he was going to walk the six-mile journey back to his home. About one and a half miles from Leeds, he called in at a pub called the Dog and Gun for one last drink. There he recognised a man he knew as Francis Clough (24) and, after finishing their drinks, they decided that they would walk the remaining distance together. On his person, Whitehead had eight £5 notes, two sovereigns and 12s in silver coins. When they reached a part of the road beside the lodge of Killingbeck Hall, they saw James Brooksbank (25) and William Ayrton (23). They men said 'good evening' as they passed and Whitehead and Clough carried on walking for about 100 yards, when Clough suddenly seized Whitehead and threw him to the ground. Ayrton and Brooksbank then ran back and joined in with the attack on Whitehead. One of the robbers emptied Whitehead's pockets while the others held him down on the ground. After rifling his pockets the men ran off leaving the injured man in the road. Thankfully he managed to stagger to his feet and get to the safety of his home, where the police were called. The three robbers were later all seen together in a public house at about 9 p.m., where it was noted that Ayrton paid the barman in silver coins. He was arrested, but when the police tried to arrest Clough the next day at Leeds, he put up considerable resistance. Whilst he was struggling with an officer, he was seen to put something in his mouth, which later proved to be two of the £5 bank notes taken during the robbery. When Brooksbank attempted to change one of the stolen bank notes, he also was arrested and charged with highway robbery. The three men were brought to the Assizes in March 1840, where the jury found all three guilty and sentenced them to be transported for life.

Highway robbers and their victim (*Tales of the Terrific Register: The Book of London*)

Even with the prospect of the criminals spending the rest of their lives in another country, the authorities were determined to split up this gang of highway robbers. Francis Clough was the first to be transported on the *Asia* on 25 April 1840, bound for Van Diemen's Land. Broadbent was the next to go; he left on the *Eden* on 8 July 1840, heading for New South Wales, and William Ayrton was the last to leave, on the *Lady Raffles,* on 30 November 1840, also bound for Van Diemen's Land.

On 14 October 1844, three audacious robbers were caught at Yarm (NR) after robbing a farmer of the proceeds from selling some cattle. A Mr Harland sold twenty-nine cattle and was paid £185 for them, most of which was in Scottish £5 notes. After completing his business, he walked to a nearby public house where he had stabled his pony to return home. Before he reached the public house, he was approached by a woman who put her arms around him. Harland tried to shake her off, but she tore open his waistcoat and stole his pocket book containing the notes. When he went to get them back she was joined by two other men who attacked him and knocked him to the ground.

When the three people had left, he called a constable and the two men searched the area. They found his empty pocket book and some strings from a cloak which had been worn by the woman when the robbery was being committed. The next day, Harland was asked to identify three people and he confirmed they were the ones who had committed the robbery. The woman was called Sarah Wilson, aged twenty-three, and she was known to have gone to Yarm with two men, who were Thomas Addy and Christopher Ingledew, both aged twenty-nine. The numbers of the notes were checked and it was confirmed that they came from a sequence of notes paid out to Harland. However, at the trial the defence made some allusion to the fact that Harland had said that he wasn't sure it was the right woman. The judge made it clear to the jury that they had to make sure Wilson was the woman who had committed the crime, as the case against the others would fall down if they were unsure. But the jury took only three quarters of an hour to find all three of the prisoners guilty. Addy and Ingledew were sentenced to two years' imprisonment but Sarah Wilson, who was seen as inciting the two men to commit the crime, received a harder sentence. She was transported on the convict ship *Lloyd* on 23 July 1845 for seven years in Van Diemen's Land. The life for women transportees was as harsh a regime as for men. They would have to work in factories or as domestic servants for the amount of their sentence, although many married and remained abroad to bring up their children.

In another case, a woman was, again, used as a decoy for highway robbers. On Friday, 21 December 1860 the court of the York Assizes were told about the robbery of Mr George Green of Barnsley (WR). The two prisoners at the bar were Elizabeth Ann Lyons (20), and George Shaw (32). Green had been an innkeeper at Hemsworth and had gone into Barnsley to conduct some business. Whilst in the town he called in to the Butcher's Arms public house where he met some friends and stayed with them for about an hour. On leaving the pub, he was accosted by Lyons, but, as he tried to push her away, a man appeared and knocked him to the ground. Whilst he lay on the floor struggling with the man, another man intervened, putting his foot on Green's head and threatening to 'crush his brains out'. At this point he saw Lyons rifling through his pockets and stealing twelve sovereigns before the trio ran away. Green managed to call a constable and gave an account of the robbery and described the three robbers. So accurate was his description that, within a very short period, Shaw and Lyons had been arrested, although the third man was never identified. It was reported that the constable had arrested Shaw because he noted, 'His coat and hat were muddy and he gave the impression of a man who had been struggling with another on the ground.' When Lyons had been arrested and searched at the police station she was found to have nine sovereigns and some silver still in her possession. The defence stated that it was a case of mistaken identity with Shaw and several witnesses gave evidence as to his respectability. The judge summed up the case for the jury and they brought back a verdict of not guilty for Shaw. Lyons, who had a previous conviction for robbery, was sentenced to four years at the Wakefield House of Correction.

A most curious case came before a judge at the Assizes held at the Crown Court at York in December 1865, when the jury was told of highway robbery being committed by a blind man. The man named John Cuddy (22) had pleaded not guilty to assaulting William Eley and stealing a watch from him at Bradford (WR) on 7 October 1865. It seems that Mr Eley was walking to Halifax late at night and, not knowing the way, asked a night watchman to direct him. Cuddy was standing nearby and offered to show him the way as he was also travelling along that road. The two men walked quite a long way until Cuddy told his companion that he knew of a shortcut across Wibsey Common. They proceeded to go across the common when Eley began to get suspicious as there was no obvious road and the surrounded countryside was quite deserted. He insisted on going back to the road that they had left and continuing with their journey. It was at this point that Cuddy knocked him to the floor, and stole his watch, yanking it so hard that the chain broke off in his hand. Leaving Eley senseless on the floor Cuddy made haste towards Leeds where he later tried to pawn the watch for 4s. Unfortunately, there were not too many blind highway robbers around; Cuddy was soon arrested and sent to take his trial at the Leeds Assizes on Saturday 16 December, before Mr Justice Shee. The court was told that Cuddy was well known in Bradford, where he made his way around the town without assistance of any kind. Medical evidence was given to the jury to state that the man was all but completely blind. Cuddy told the court that he had bought the watch off Eley for 2s 6d during their journey together, but Eley had regretted it and taken the watch back. Cuddy stated that it was for that reason that he had knocked him down in order to recover the watch. The judge, whilst summing up, expressed astonishment that a man who was unable to see could conduct himself and another over hedges and fields. The jury found him guilty and he was sentenced to twelve months' imprisonment with hard labour. The man showed no repentance and told the judge as he left the dock, 'It is a bad jury My Lord. I hope they know what it is to be blind before they die,' before being led away to the cells.

These then were some of the highway robbers that lurked in the country roads and the towns and cities of Yorkshire, preying on honest people. They were as far removed from the legendary highwaymen John 'Swift Nick' Nevison and Dick Turpin as they could be. Sometimes their booty was as small as a watch and a few shillings, but they all suffered imprisonment or transportation for their sins.

Chapter Two

Riots and Treason

The villains in this chapter might well be seen to some local people as heroes who stood up for the rights of the common man. Historically, Yorkshire men have not been afraid to rebel against the highest authority, as the Yorkshire rebellion of 1489 and the Pilgrimage of Grace in 1536 will testify. The tracts of open moorlands in Yorkshire were suitable for holding large open-air meetings. Groups of policemen or soldiers could be seen approaching for miles, which allowed time for political activists to disappear and remain free. During this period, legal authorities feared revolution and, therefore, made an effort to crack down on such law breakers. These 'villains' were charged with a variety of offences, from sedition to high treason, and the resulting heavy punishments were meant as a deterrent to others. As a consequence, there were times when the Castle Prison at York was so overcrowded that extra soldiers were employed to keep the peace within the prison itself.

By 1810, great strides had been made in industry and particularly in the mills and factories of Yorkshire. Machines were developed which would do the work of several men, and not unnaturally there was as lot of opposition to the installation of these machines. These men were stirred into action by someone given the mythical name of Ned Ludd and they became known as Luddites, a word which still exists in our vocabulary today.

The activities of these groups of men were frowned upon by the local authorities and great attempts were made to stamp them out. Attacks on machinery had been held in Nottinghamshire, Leicestershire and Lancashire and by 1812, the rioting had spread to Yorkshire. Such was the fear of revolution that the government in February 1812 ordered that the crime of machine breaking become a capital offence. In the area around Huddersfield, one group of Luddites were led by an educated man who was a cloth dresser known as George Mellor. On the night of 11 April 1812, Mellor, with a group of over 100 men, led them in an attack on Rawfolds Mill near Brighouse (WR). All the men were armed with weapons of varying descriptions to smash machinery at the mill. The owner of the mill was a man named William Cartwright, who was expecting trouble and had provided an armed guard to protect his mill that night. In the rioting which followed, two of the Luddites were mortally wounded.

Seven days later, Mellor led the attack on William Horsfall's mill at Marsden near Huddersfield (WR). But Horsefall, who was another large industrialist in the area, also had his mill well guarded and the Luddites were unable to penetrate it. On Tuesday, 26 April 1812, a trap was set to kill Horsefall on his way home from Huddersfield to Marsden. He was travelling with another local manufacturer named Mr Eastwood, when approximately a mile and a half from the town, he noted some pistol barrels pointing out from small holes in walls at each side of the road. Before he could escape, all four guns went off at once and he fell to the ground, senseless. Four men were later seen running away as Horsefall was being taken to a nearby inn. Three quarters of an hour later, a troop of dragoons had been assembled to join in with the search of the surrounding area for the four men. Large rewards were offered for the capture of the men or anyone involved in machine breaking. As a result of information being received, almost 100 Yorkshire men were arrested. Many were released as there was not enough evidence against them; nevertheless the Calendar of Felons records that in January 1813 there was over sixty men awaiting trial in York Castle Prison. Among those who were on trial were William Thorpe (23), and Thomas Smith (22), both of Huddersfield, and the leader George Mellor

(22), of Longroyd Bridge. The men were charged with 'aiding and assisting in the attack on William Cartwright's Mill, and being concerned in the murder of William Horsfall'. It became obvious that their trial, which took place on 2 January 1813, was intended to be a 'show trial' – where the legal authorities were not primarily concerned with justice. During the trial, the prosecution bullied and harried witnesses. But the Huddersfield Luddites knew the end had come when one of their gang turned Queen's evidence against them. Mellor, Thorpe and Smith were sentenced to be hanged on Friday 8 January and their bodies were to be dissected. The short time period between the trial and the execution meant that the authorities had given the men no time to appeal against their sentence. Such was the sympathy for these so-called villains that when the hanging took place at York, it was noted that although a very large crowd was present they were completely silent. Eight days later, another fourteen rioters took their trial, charged with 'tumultuously assembling in the night time to destroy shearing frames and machinery, to collect fire arms and to demolish mills'. Three of the prisoners were acquitted and others were discharged. However, five men, James Haigh (28), Jonathon Dean (30), John Ogden (28), John Walker and Thomas Brook (both 31), were all found guilty and sentenced to death. They ascended the scaffold outside York Castle on Saturday, 16 January 1813 singing the hymn 'Behold the Saviour of Mankind', before being launched into eternity.

Great economic hardships caused the weavers of the same areas of West Riding to riot and make demands for political reform a few years later. The rebellion was exacerbated by the thousands of men returning home after the end of the Napoleonic Wars, which resulted in pre-Chartists groups demanding universal male suffrage. A public meeting had been held at Barnsley (WR) in May 1819, where hundreds of people demanded reform. When they were denied this, more militant action was taken in what became known as the Yorkshire Rebellion of 1820. The hand weavers of the West Riding were rapidly becoming more politicised through their collective poverty – they demanded action. Many of these political groups wanted their demands to be heard through Parliament, whereas more radical groups wanted nothing

The site of the gallows at York. (Courtesy of Richard Stansfield)

less than revolution. A plan was outlined to attack; on 31 March 1820, the radicals were to attempt to take control of the 'lightly defended' town of Huddersfield. Four large groups consisting of hundreds of men marched on Huddersfield, chanting slogans to the effect that 'the revolution starts tonight'. The local authorities were forewarned and a dragoon of guards was assembled at the George Inn, Huddersfield. For some unknown reason, the storming of the town was called off and men slipped away quietly to their own homes. Despite the fact that no blood had been shed, the authorities were determined to treat these rioters with the utmost severity. On Saturday, 15 July 1820, ten men were brought to York prison on charges of rioting and high treason. They were:

Thomas Blackburn (33)
Nathan Buckley (40)
John Lindley (50)
William Comstive (28)
Richard Addey (29)
Charles Stanfield (28)
Benjamin Hanson (24)
Abraham Ingham (27)
George Brien (26)
John Hobson (20)

They were all charged ; it was said that, 'together with other people alleged to be more than 500-strong, they traitorously assembled together for the purpose of levying public war against Our Sovereign Lord the King and against his peace'. Blackburn, Buckley, Ingham, Brien and Hobson were sent to the prison hulks for two years. Lindley and Comstive were transported for fourteen years and the rest were sentenced to seven years' transportation.

But if the West Riding authorities hoped that this would spell the end of the rebellions across the Yorkshire region, they were wrong. These early rebellions were just the forerunner for the Chartists, who took their name from the People's Charter, which demanded reform of the voting system. The Reform Act of 1832 had given the vote to a number of middle class voters, but the working classes were now demanding equal votes. By 1838, a group made up of working people and Members of Parliament drew up the People's Charter, which struck a chord in the minds of working class people. Once again, the government was faced with revolution as meetings of hundreds of people gathered in the more remote parts of Yorkshire. On 15 October 1838, a large meeting was held on Hartshead Moor, near Leeds, which was judged to be equidistant from the West Riding towns of Bradford, Halifax, Barnsley and Huddersfield. The place where the meeting was held was a natural amphitheatre, and was well attended by people not only demanding reform, but also with markets stalls, which gave the site a fairground-like quality. Speeches were heard urging that nothing would be changed unless it could be taken by force. In June 1839, a petition had been presented to the House of Commons which had been refused, and this single act caused the groups of Chartists all over the Yorkshire area to take military action.

In the beginning of January 1840, it was decided by a group of Sheffield Chartists (WR) to gather arms and take over the Town Hall and the Tontine Inn by force, and fortify them against the militia, which they knew would be called out. The revolt in Sheffield was supposed to have been part of an uprising of the whole country between Saturday 11 and Sunday 12 January. In order to achieve their aims, the men were prepared to set fire to the town. But the magistrates had been warned, possibly by spies employed by the police, to attend Chartist meetings and report back to them. Orders were given to arrest the ringleaders: Samuel Holberry, Thomas Booker, William Booker, John Clayton, Samuel Bentley, John Marshall, Thomas Penthorpe, Joseph Bennison and William Wells were all arrested and brought to the Assizes on 21 March 1840 – all were accused of seditious conspiracy. This also was intended to be a show trial which was demonstrated by the prominent display of baskets of hand grenades in the courtroom, as well as pikes and pistols which had been used in the attack. Holberry informed the judge that he was the leader and willing participant and – rather than denying his part in the uprising – swore that he would 'die for the Charter'. The main body of evidence against them was given by two men – Samuel Foxhall and Samuel Powell Thompson, who had taken part in the riots but had turned Queen's evidence.

It seems that Sheffield Chartists had been planning the riot during their meetings at a house in Fig Tree Lane. To carry out their plan, Holberry had instructed the men to meet at Sheffield Town Hall and the Tontine Inn, 'exactly as the clock strikes 2 a.m.' It was estimated that there would be over 200 armed men. Those men without arms were instructed to break into gunsmiths and take what was required. It was agreed that when they took possession of the Tontine, a coaching inn, they were to barricade

Sheffield Town Hall. (Courtesy of Picture Sheffield)

themselves in using any coaches that were already in the yard. Those who broke into the Town Hall had to be split into two; one force to overpower anyone upstairs and one force to do the same downstairs. Sharp implements known as 'cats' were to be thrown on Snig Hill, which was a hill between the police station and the barracks, in order to prevent the horses from entering the town. The remainders of the Chartists were instructed to assassinate all the night watchmen they came across. The evidence against the men was so strong that Judge Erskine had little problem in directing the jury to find all the men 'guilty of seditious conspiracy for the purpose of obstructing the law and for making riots and disturbing the public peace'.

The men were sentenced the following week on 5 March 1840, where the judge told them that the jury might be justified in coming to the conclusion that they had 'levied war against the Queen and were therefore guilty of high treason'. He stated that, as Englishmen, they had a right to their own opinions, but this was not the case, however, when they procured arms for unlawful purposes; they were found guilty of high treason. Samuel Holberry was sentenced to four years at the Northallerton House of Correction, and the other Chartists received various prison sentences from one to three years. A petition was started demanding that the Sheffield Chartists, and particularly Holberry, be released. The conditions in prison at that time were terrible, and it was not long before Holberry was returned to York Castle Prison hospital in a very weak condition. He was brought to the castle on 21 September 1841, and he died on the morning of 21 June 1842; an inquest was held the same day which went into the details of his last illness. The Deputy Governor, Mr Baxter Barker, told the coroner that he had received notice of a full pardon for Holberry, dated 17 June 1842, but he had died before he could be released. The verdict of the coroner's jury was that he died 'by a visitation of God'. He was seen by the Sheffield people as being one of the first Chartist martyrs and was buried in Sheffield on Monday 27 June with great ceremony. It was attended by hundreds of people.

Such was the popularity of the Chartist movement and the support from the working classes that, once again, it was feared by the authorities that it would trigger off a national revolt.

The Governor of York Castle Prison kept a journal in which he logged the daily events as well as the number of prisoners received into the gaol. In his diary on 21 August 1842, he records, 'As a consequence of there being many Chartists in the city, I have given notice to the porter not to admit any but relatives.' There was a real fear that Chartists may take it upon themselves to storm the castle and release the prisoners. To prevent that from happening, the military was called in the following week. The Governor noted that, 'the militia conducted themselves very well and the prisoners were quiet but nevertheless, there were 266 out of which 119 had been convicted of rioting from the West Riding.'

On the 23 August, more Chartists from Leeds had been admitted to the prison, and on the 27 August he noted, 'There were then 145 rioters for trial who were guarded by privates and one sergeant.' Thankfully, by 5 September 1842, all the rioters had been sentenced. Eighteen had been liberated on their own recognisances of good behaviour, one had been transported and the others were sentenced to imprisonment at the Wakefield House of Correction for different periods of time. He noted, 'The military have now been dismissed'.

Two weeks after the Sheffield Chartist rising took place, a similar riot was planned in Bradford (WR) on Sunday 26 and Monday, 27 January 1840. A meeting had been held the previous week where two men, Robert Peddie and William Brook (both 37), formulated a plan to take possession of the town. It was agreed that they would go to Low Moor Ironworks, owned by Messrs Dawson and Hardy, an iron manufacturer, take possession of a cannon and use it to storm the town. Another group was to do the same at Dewsbury and other towns across the West Riding. All the groups would then join together and march to London in order to take possession of the government.

Peddie and Brook agreed to meet the other Chartists at 2 a.m. on the morning of Sunday 26 January at Lidgett Green, near Bradford. The different groups were instructed to bring arms with them and to congregate outside a shop named Smiths, from where they would proceed into the town centre. The first time it was brought to the attention of the police was when they were told that armed men were walking around the streets of Bradford

Snig Hill, Sheffield.
(Courtesy of Picture
Sheffield)

The Gaoler's Journal.
(Courtesy of City
of York Council
Archives and Local
History)

for unlawful purposes. It was also reported that a night watchman, one Thomas Croft, had been kidnapped and imprisoned in a shed at the bottom of the garden of Mr John Crabtree at the Market Tavern Inn, Bradford. His watchman's rattle had been taken away from him and, a short time later, he was joined by another watchman, one William Illingworth. It was reported that the shed had been guarded by men carrying long pikes and pistols. The Bradford magistrates instructed a group of watchmen to take a party of special constables and release the two imprisoned watchmen. A larger group was sent out to round up the Chartists roaming around the town. They encountered a group of men near the Bradford Dispensary who were holding pikes, guns and other weapons. Some were taken and arrested but many others ran away. It was reported that, unlike the organised military action of the Sheffield Chartists, the whole proceedings were done so quietly that many inhabitants of the town had no idea that anything was taking place. However, on Monday it was reported that there was 'a great sense of excitement in the town and the courthouse looked like a place under siege, with a 6lb cannon in front and a large posse of constables in and around the place'. A large placard had been erected which was placed outside the courthouse, stating that the magistrates:

> call upon all well disposed persons to assist them in the preservation of the public peace and not to be out except on urgent business after eight o'clock. At which hour they require all public houses and beer houses to be closed.

Later that morning, the ten prisoners were brought before the bench at the Bradford Courthouse on 10 February 1840. They were Peddie and Brook, Thomas Drake, Phineas Smithies, John Walker, Joseph Naylor, John Ashton, Emmanuel Hutton, John Riding, Francis Rushworth and James and Paul Holdsworth. Once again, the courtroom displayed several pikes, muskets, bayonets and daggers which had been taken from the prisoners following their arrest. Peddie, Brook, Drake and Paul Holdsworth were charged with treason whilst another ten men were charged with riot and conspiracy. The men were brought in to the courtroom in small groups to be tried by the magistrates. Peddie and Brook were tried first and both men were found guilty and ordered to take their trial at the York Assizes. The proceedings, which took most of the day, resulted in all the men being found guilty. At the end of the day, all the prisoners were sent in a coach to York Castle and such was the support for the Chartists that they were accompanied by a party of Hussars for safekeeping.

Despite the popularity of these political activists, it was reported that the appearance of all the prisoners were 'wretched in the extreme'. By the time they were brought to the Assizes on 5 March 1840, the prosecution made fun of the fact that a dozen men were prepared to storm Bradford and then take on the government. But the judge summed up the evidence against the men and the jury took only fifteen minutes to find all guilty. Sentencing was deferred until the following week when the judge, before issuing his sentence, told them that:

> The exercise of force introduces a system of anarchy, confusion and disorder. They render the name of Chartism odious by the violent means they use to carry into effect the principles they profess.

Peddie was sentenced to three years' imprisonment with hard labour at Beverley House of Correction, Brook three years at Northallerton, Drake eighteen months' imprisonment at Beverley, and Holdsworth three years at Northallerton. The remainder of the Chartists were given twelve months' hard labour at Northallerton.

The Chartists movement was popular in the Yorkshire area. Similar uprisings were experienced in other towns of West Yorkshire at the same time and all were dealt with severely by the legal authorities. Yet despite the harsh sentences, thousands of Yorkshire people had rallied together to demand Parliamentary Reforms and hundreds were sent to prison and transported for their beliefs. While they were regarded as villains by the majority of the magistrates and other legal authorities, the cases show that these men were very brave – all were prepared to suffer for their affiliation to Chartism.

Chapter Three

Forgery and Counterfeiting

Up until 1830, forgery was a seen as a capital crime which could result in a death sentence or transportation. The authorities were aware that the crime of altering wills or forging documents for the purpose of fraud and deception would result in de-stabilising the economy, thereby causing chaos. This was made more complicated by the fact that many banks issued their own bank notes, which were not all Bank of England notes like we have today. The crime of forgery also encompassed counterfeiting or 'coining' – making false coins from diluted metals in moulds. The possession of either fraudulent documents or coins would result in a prison sentence. In legal terms, the act of passing on these false coins or banknotes was called 'uttering'. The Calendar of Felons, dated 8 March 1800, lists a couple named Sarah Bailey and John McWilliams, who were both hanged at York on Saturday, 12 April 1800 for the crime of 'uttering forged notes' at Sheffield. Other cases of forgery involved signing another person's name on a bill or banker's order without their permission.

Thankfully, by the middle of the nineteenth century, sentences for forgery or counterfeiting were becoming less serious. One such case was heard on Saturday, 30 November 1844 when the fool-hardy behaviour of a man from Thirsk (NR) was heard at the York Assizes. The man known as Thomas Carter (a.k.a. James Foster) was charged with uttering a banker's order for £13 on 20 July, with the intention of defrauding the Yorkshire District Banking Company at Thirsk. On 29 July he had repeated the offence with another order for £20. The forged order was 'signed' by Christopher Sadler – a brewer who lived at Thornton le Moor, near Thirsk. The bank had a branch office at Thirsk; it was commonly known that Mr Saddler did business there. On 20 July, Carter, who was a labourer, asked the manager, William Johnson, if Mr Saddler was in the bank and he replied that he wasn't. Carter told him that he had spoken to Mr Saddler at 10 a.m. that morning and had arranged to meet him at the bank. He also told the manager that if Mr Saddler wasn't there, he had to present a letter. The letter stated:

Thornton le Moor
20 July 1844

To Mr Johnson
Yorkshire District Bank
Thirsk

Please pay to James Jackson the sum of £13 by order of Christopher Saddler. I shall see you on Monday

Your Obliged Servant
Christopher Saddler

Carter told the manager that he had sold some barley to Mr Saddler for £13 and he had assured him that the bank would pay. Mr Johnson remembered that Saddler had recently ceased to be a brewer, and was suspicious of the letter, so he asked Carter if his name was Jackson – he told him that it was. The manager asked him to return in half an hour, and, in the meantime, established that the letter was a forgery. Despite the fact that Carter had a near miss, incredibly he then went back to the bank a second time on 29 July with another letter, once again purporting to be from Saddler, stating:

Mr Johnson – Sir – would you be so kind as to send by the bearer the sum of £20, as I am so poorly that I cannot come myself. I have sent my man James Foster and I will come on Wednesday or Thursday, if all is well.

Christopher Saddler

This time the manager knew that Carter was not James Foster and he was seized and searched. On his person, they found similar orders for money addressed to the Bedale and Wensleydale Banks also supposedly from Saddler. The prisoner then began to cry and pleaded with Johnson to let him go, but a constable was called and he was arrested and charged. His defence told the jury that Carter had been instructed to present the orders by an unnamed man and that he was merely following orders. The jury returned a verdict of guilty and he was given a sentence of two years in prison.

Another curious case involved a mother who committed forgery on her son at Beverley (NR). The case was heard at the York Assizes in March 1848, but there occured an unusual twist. On 20 February, a woman named Sarah Elizabeth Clubley had produced a paper which she gave to the manager of the Beverley Savings Bank. She stated that her son had written it in order to allow her to be able to take money out of his account by proxy. The manager looked at the paper carefully, but, upon finding nothing wrong, allowed her to take out £2. Her son, Joseph Clubley, was a depositor at the bank and he knew the regulations. He demanded that if he was to send another person to take money out of his account, an appointment of proxy had to be produced bearing the signature of the depositor and two witnesses.

Joseph Clubley denied writing the appointment of proxy and Mrs Clubley was arrested and sent before the magistrates. She told them that the forgery had been done by a man named John Lockwood Haigh. Haigh had asked a witness named Wright to sign the paper but when he expressed reluctance, Haigh told him it was merely a document allowing him to go into the country and no harm would come to him in consequence of him doing so. Reluctantly, Wright had done as he was requested. When the case came to York Assizes on Saturday, 18 March 1848, Haigh told the court that the forgery had been done at the request of Mrs Clubley.

The judge summed up for the jury and at his direction, John Haigh was found not guilty and discharged. Before the jury could

The lawyer's table in
the courtroom.

pronounce a verdict on the mother, Mrs Clubley's son appeared and
told the judge that his mother had paid the £2 to defray his tailor's
bill. No doubt thinking that the woman could not be discharged for
a crime of which she was clearly guilty, the judge ordered that she be
imprisoned in the women's prison at the castle for a week until the
end of the Assizes.

A more serious case was heard at on the 5 December 1859 when
a man was charged with forging a will. A widow, one Ann Buckle,
was the proprietor of the New Inn at Askham Richard (NR),
which was situated between York and Tadcaster. Her nephew,
William Stockdale (35), had lived with her for many years and
had conducted much of the business of the inn. Two days before
she died, in March 1859, Stockdale contacted her firm of solicitors, stating that she wanted to alter the will and asked that one of
them attend her at the inn. Mr T.L. Bickers Esq. of Tadcaster was
dispatched to her home but found her too weak and ill to make
any alterations. When she died, her original will was read out to
the relatives of the deceased woman and at that time no one made

Women's prison, York Castle. (Courtesy of York Museum Trust)

any objections to the contents. Stockdale stated, however, that he wished to purchase and continue running the inn and notices were put up around the town notifying people of the sale. A purchaser was soon found to be Mr John Smith, a brewer at Tadcaster, whose business still exists today. He bought the property on 22 June 1860 for the price of £475. Immediately before the sale, Stockdale had issued notices around the town asking people not to buy the property as he stated, 'It rightfully belongs to me and therefore it is not for sale.' It seems that he had contacted a firm of solicitors on 27 May 1859 to say that another will had been written by his aunt on the 4 September 1858. In the new will, she had left the whole of the property to him and therefore the property should not have been sold. He could not explain why he had made no objections to the will which had been read out to the deceased relatives at the time.

An investigation was undertaken when it became clear that the new will had been forged. The police found that the forged will had been written by a Mr Walmsley of Hutton, a former solicitor, on the understanding that it was for Mrs Buckle and at the request of Stockdale. At the time, Stockdale had approached two local businessmen to ask if they would witness the will but they refused. He then requested his father-in-law, Dennis Coates (74), and neighbour, John Coates (37), to sign the will as witnesses. Stockdale was brought to the Assizes in December 1860 and was charged with 'uttering a false will knowing it to be forged, with intent to defraud'. Both Coates were charged with 'aiding and abetting Stockdale in the committal of the said offence'. The judge, after hearing all the evidence, pointed out that no person would be safe in disposing of their property by will if such a case was to remain unpunished, and he sentenced Stockdale to six years' penal servitude and the two Coates to one month in prison each.

The uttering of coins or banks notes was a crime which was more often than not committed by women. Perhaps it was thought that women would be more likely to get away with it or would receive a lesser sentence than a man. At a later Assizes in August of the same year, two people were charged with uttering forged Bank of England notes at Selby (NR) on 10 August 1860. The two people were Fanny Leave (19), who was charged with uttering the notes, and William Bateman (alias Richardson) who was charged with 'counselling Leave to commit the offence'. On the day in question, Leave went into the grocer's shop of a Mr Lee at Selby and asked him to change a £5 note, foolishly telling him that she had been to five or six different shops and had been unable to cash it. Mr Lee examined it carefully and agreed that he would change the note for her. He put the £5 note on one side and he later found out that it was indeed forged. Meanwhile, Leave had been watched by Superintendent Lotty of the Selby police force, who had previously seen her in the company of Bateman and another man. He thought that they were acting suspiciously when he witnessed him giving her something, although he was unable to see what it was.

When she came out of Mr Lee's shop, Lotty approached her and asked to see the £5 note as he was aware that she had been trying to change it in other shops. She denied having any such note in her possession, but he told her that she had to accompany him to the police station. On the way he noticed her putting something into her mouth, and, on reaching the station, he forced her mouth open to find a second forged £5 Bank of England note. Bateman was also arrested and they were taken before the magistrate, who found them guilty. They were sent to York Assizes where the case was heard on Wednesday, 12 December 1860. The prosecution maintained that the couple had acted in unison to commit the crime; the jury agreed and both were found guilty. Before sentencing, the judge told the court that Bateman had a previous offense of exchanging a £10 note at another shop in Selby, and because of this he gave him a sentence of ten years' penal servitude. Probably due to the fact that it was Leave's first offence, and, given her very young age, the judge was more lenient and sentenced her to only three years in prison.

An isolated farmhouse, situated in the moors above Halifax, contained a family of forgers in December of 1842 that were found to be so successful, they appeared to have their own bank. The discovery of the crime started when a man named William Lawton Smith was taken into custody for having in his possession a forged banknote belonging to the Wirksworth, Ashbourne and Derbyshire Bank.

After making a voluntary statement to the Leeds police superintendent, Mr James, a raid on Holden's farm was made. Smith told Mr James that he had been at the farm in May 1842 and the elder Mr Holden had shown him a box containing a quantity of banknotes. He had stated that the only thing missing from the bank note was the signature of Mr Frederick Arkwright, a senior bank official. He told Mr James that the senior Holden had his grandson at the farm at the time, a man named William Barrett, who worked in a solicitor's office. Holden asked Barrett to sign the name as near to the original, which he also had in his possession, and he did so. He also signed another thirty or forty bank notes for them, and in return was given fourteen of the notes. Following Smith's statement, Mr James ordered that an early morning raid be held on the farm where John Holden (73) lived with his sons John, the younger (40). Zachariah (37), Thomas (36), James (29) and his daughter Betty (32). Aware that they would be spotted if they went in daylight, the raid took place at 6.30 a.m. The door was answered by Thomas the younger, who, when asked where his father was, stated that he was not at home. Searching the property, the officers found in a hay loft a parcel wrapped up in a piece of damask. The parcel contained a copper plate made for the purpose of producing the forged banknotes. They then searched the house where they found a tin box in which was placed several more forged bank notes. There were twenty-one notes purporting to be from the Wirksworth, Ashbourne and Derbyshire banks, together with ten other notes, supposedly from the Halifax and Huddersfield bank.

The prisoners were all taken to the police station with the exception of the older man and the girl. Whilst on his way to Halifax, the younger John Holden boasted to the officers, 'Well you have broken our bank at last.'

'Yes,' the officer replied.

Holden then said, 'You didn't think there was a bank in this part of the country did you?'

The same day, a representative of the Halifax and Huddersfield bank went back to the farmhouse with some more officers and searched the house more thoroughly. They found a purse belonging to Betty Holden and inside were small metal letters which had been used on the bank notes. The items were confiscated and the prisoners charged and bailed at the Halifax Magistrates' Court until their appearance in the York Assizes in March 1843. The serious nature of the trial was noted by a reporter who stated that the villains had been 'an infamous and extensive gang whose forgeries were not just confined to provincial banks but to the Bank of England itself'.

A typically isolated farmhouse, located in the moors above Halifax.
(Courtesy of Sue Trickey)

The family was brought before the court on two charges. On the first charge the judge condemned the fact that Smith had been brought from Nottingham jail to give evidence, but had then been prevented from doing so by the prosecution. The judge used 'very strong language' to make his displeasure known. After hearing all the evidence, the jury passed a guilty verdict on both John Holden senior and junior, but the rest were found not guilty and discharged. The second charge was also against John Holden senior, Zachariah and John Holden the younger, and William Barrett. On this occasion, William Lawton Smith was allowed to give his evidence and he told the court that he was now serving a sentence in Nottingham jail for trying to pass one of the forged bank notes. He gave his evidence but when the prisoner was dismissed, the defence suggested that the copper plate found on the premises of the farmhouse 'might have been deposited there by that fellow' (meaning Smith). He claimed that if the jury agreed, then the prisoners should be given a verdict of not guilty. The jury agreed regarding Zachariah and William Barrett, but they found both John Holden senior and junior guilty of the crime of forgery. There was no doubt that, as the two older members of the gang, they were seen to be the most culpable, and the following day the judge sentenced both to transportation. The younger Holden was transported for life, leaving England on the *Maitland* on 26 August 1843. The elder Holden, no doubt due to his age, was merely given seven years transportation. He left on the *London* on 15 March 1844; both were bound for Van Diemen's Land.

During this period, there were many villains known as 'coiners' who clipped coins which were usually made of silver or gold. The edges of original coins made of silver or gold would be clipped and the corners, using the clippings and coloured metals, would make additional coins. As we have seen more often than not, coiners would have women 'utter' the counterfeit coins in the towns of Yorkshire. Busy shopkeepers were not always able to inspect the proffered coins and they were the easiest to dupe and consequently were the most targeted by coiners.

A woman named Ann Green (27) was found to be guilty of uttering counterfeit coins on 31 October 1843 in Leeds (WR), where she was charged with 'giving a forged shilling to Rachel

Kennedy knowing it to be counterfeit'. She also gave another one to shopkeeper named Lockwood Hurst. At the Assizes held on 16 December 1843 at York, she was found guilty on the two counts. She also had a previous charge of uttering made against her and as a consequence she was sentenced to be transported for ten years. At York Castle, the Governor noted that on 3 July 1843 he had sent fourteen female prisoners to Millbank Prison ready for transportation, and the group included Ann. She had wanted to take her daughter (6) with her, which had been agreed, but unfortunately on the journey south, her daughter was taken ill. When she arrived at Millbank the prison surgeon returned the child back to York. He stated that Ann could not take the child with her out of the country, but if her mother sent for her they would try to get her to visit before the ship sailed. Ann Green was transported on the *Angelina* in the company of 250 other female convicts on 25 April 1844, to serve out her sentence in Van Diemen's Land.

There were some cases of couples working together to pass on counterfeit coins. Two such people were arrested in Sheffield (WR) in 1865, charged with uttering coins in the local shops of the town: Thomas Holland and Elizabeth Thompson (both 19). They were found guilty and sent to the Leeds Assizes to take their trial on Saturday 16 December before Mr Justice Shee. On 8 November, Holland was busy visiting shops in the town buying small items with the counterfeit coins. It was reported that he went into a greengrocer shop run by a Mrs Wyatt and bought a pound of pears, for which he gave a florin (2s). Mrs Wyatt had no change so she asked her own little girl to run to Mrs Ewalls a nearby grocer and get it changed. The girl did as she was requested and the change was given to Holland.

A short time later, Mrs Ewalls told Mrs Wyatt that she thought the coin was counterfeit and she was going to take it to the police. In fact, her husband gave it to Detective Cornwall at the Sheffield Town Hall. A few days later, Holland went into the shop of Mrs Evans, a hosier of Broomhall Street, and bought two ounces of scarlet wool, once again giving her a florin to pay for it. Mrs Evans suspected that it was counterfeit and challenged him, but he denied it. Not trusting him, she put the coin in a separate compartment in the till. Once again, the coin was found to be counterfeit and was taken to the police at the Town Hall. Detective Cornwall took both coins to a watchmaker and jeweller on West Bar for analysis. They were proved to be made from white metal and zinc which had been heated and placed in a mould. The two prisoners were later seen together and arrested. Thompson admitted to having been found guilty of uttering a half crown coin in Sheffield on 5 November. She pleaded guilty to that charge, but protested that she did not know anything about Holland offering false coins on 8 November. She claimed that she was innocent and at the time he was committing the offences she was at home. The judge summed up the case for the jury and they were both found guilty. His Lordship sentenced her to eighteen months' imprisonment with hard labour but he warned her that if she was brought before the court again for a similar offence, she would receive a sentence of seven years in prison. Holland was sentenced to twelve months with hard labour, as it was felt by the jury that he was the instigator of the crime.

The crime of coining continued throughout the nineteenth century. Later, coins had ridges made on the side of them to prevent this from happening. Even today there are letters around a £1 coin that read '*Decus et tutamen*', which are there to indicate whether a coin has been clipped or not. It was said at one point that there were hundreds of coiners in operation in Yorkshire, but these have just been a few of them.

Chapter Four

Stealing

There is little doubt that the most common crime heard at the York and Leeds Assizes was that of stealing. Today, theft is a minor offence and most would get away relatively unscathed with a fine or a caution, but, in the nineteenth century, as we have seen, punishments were more severe. The range of these kinds of cases varied widely and each was judged on its merit; from stealing livestock, for which you could be hanged in 1800, to stealing money or clothes. The act was, in many cases, impulsive, with little or no thought given for the consequences.

The crime of livestock stealing drew the harshest sentences during the nineteenth century. More frequently undertaken at the dead of night, smaller animals were often skinned and jointed in the field in order to prevent detection. It is probable that very few of these animals would have been found and returned back to their owners. No doubt some farmers would have turned a blind eye to one case of missing stock, but when it became a stealing spree, generally the local constables would be called in.

Two men, Richard Cooper (61) and Thomas Hall (55), from Pickering (NR) stole what was described as a 'fat ewe', the property of George Calvert on 9 November 1842. Later that same month on 24 November, they stole a wether lamb (a newly born castrated male lamb), the property of Thomas Coverdale. The two men were tried and found guilty and were sentenced at the Assizes on 6 March 1843 to be transported for fifteen years. However, before the sentence could be carried out, Cooper died in York Castle Prison. The Governor noted all incidents in his journal and on 16 March he wrote, 'Richard Cooper convicted for sheep stealing departed this life at 6 a.m.' Following the regulations, he notified the magistrate and the coroner and the inquest was held the following day at 9 a.m. Whilst giving evidence, the Governor told the coroner that before he died, Cooper told him that his father was dead, and his mother lived with a farmer at Pickering. The coroner asked him if he had informed the mother of her son's death and he said that he had written to her the previous day. Several prison officers also gave their evidence and the jury delivered a verdict that he had died through 'a visitation from God'. On 19 March, a nephew-in-law of Cooper, Mr John Hawley, came to York Castle Prison to claim the body and to take it back to Pickering to bury him there. Cooper's clothes were given to Mr Hawley and 1s, which had been found on the body, was given to one of the prisoners who tended for him in his last illness. I have

Pages of the Governor's Journal. (Courtesy of City of York Council Archives and Local History)

been unable to find any details about the transportation of his colleague in crime, Thomas Coverdale. It is to be hoped that, given the elderly ages of both men, that he might have been allowed to spend his latter years in a Yorkshire prison.

The difficulty in prosecuting such cases was indicated by a later case of horse stealing, which had been brought to the Assizes on Wednesday, 12 December 1860. A horse had been reported as stolen from Isaac and Jacob Childs at Shelly, near Huddersfield (WR) on 29 June 1859. It was described as a bay gelding that had been kept in a stable which was not locked. Twelve months later, the same gelding was found in the company of a man called Lambert, who earned his living as a carter at Bradford. The horse was identified as the one that had been stolen and the police were called in. When questioned, Lambert said that he had got the horse in an exchange for another one from a man named Richard Burton (25). Enquiries were made and it was found that Burton was at present serving a two-year prison sentence for stealing a cow and a heifer in 1859. He had also been found guilty of stealing another cow the previous year. The judge ordered that Burton have a further two years added to his sentence to be served when his present term of imprisonment ended. Burton was lucky as many of these horse thieves were transported across the seas.

Stealing from a house, shop, or public house was a much more common crime. On Tuesday, 16 February 1841, a woman was brought before the magistrates at the Leeds Courthouse charged with stealing £50 in £5 notes and some silver. Her name was Susannah Scott and she was employed by Mr John Ayrey of the Old George Inn on Briggate, Leeds (WR). At about noon on Saturday 13 February, Mr Matthew Smith, a manufacturer of Morley, asked the landlord Mr Ayrey to take care of some money for him until he was ready to go home. It was his usual habit and, as always, he gave the money in a brown paper bag to Mr Ayrey, who would lock it away in a drawer in the nursery. But being rather busy at the time, he asked his wife, who was breastfeeding the baby in the kitchen, to take it up to the nursery for him. In the meantime, he placed it in a kitchen drawer at the side of her, thinking it was safe as there were only the servants in the kitchen at the time. Mrs Ayrey was called suddenly into the bar, where she stayed only a short time before returning back to the kitchen and opening the drawer. She found it empty. A search was made but it was to no avail – the money could not be found. Two days later, handbills were distributed around the town announcing a reward of £5 for any information likely to lead to the recovery of the property and the conviction of the thief.

On the following Monday afternoon, a servant girl from a beer house in Swinegate went to the George Inn looking for Scott, stating that her mistress, Mrs Booth, wanted to see her. Scott was not there, but the publican Mr Ayrey was suspicious and he went to see Mrs Booth. He found that Scott had taken 'a brown paper parcel containing money' to Mrs Booth on the previous Saturday. Scott had told her that she had just received the money as a legacy from her aunt. Mr Ayrey asked her if she still had the parcel, but Mrs Booth told him that Scott had taken it away again the same night to a Mrs Trolly's in Ebenezer Street, Leeds. He returned to the George Inn after calling in at the police station and asked for a constable to meet them at Ebenezer Street. He then marched Scott, who had by now returned, to the house of Mrs Trolly, who produced a rosewood work box which had been given to her by Scott. The constable opened it and found £47 in the box. The money had been kept separately in parcels just as Mr Matthew Smith had wrapped them. Mrs Trolley told the constable that Scott had also given her £2 8s in loose change when she asked her to keep the box safe. The constable arrested Scott and he then took the money to Mr Matthew Smith and asked him to identify it as being the same notes that he had given to Mr Ayrey. Smith confirmed that it was the same and Scott was brought before two magistrates, Messrs Stansfield and Hebden, and committed to take her trial. When she was brought before the Assizes judge, he had little sympathy with her before sentencing her to twelve months' imprisonment at Wakefield House of Correction.

Most cases of theft were opportunist crimes committed by criminals, but the Assizes judges were shocked in 1844 when a police superintendent was brought before them accused of stealing £17. Joseph Steadman Maddison applied for and was given the job of Superintendent of Rural Police at York in 1842. The post had been created by several gentlemen who were con-

York Castle Prison. (Courtesy of York Museum Trust)

cerned about the rise of crime in York and had decided to take steps to prevent it. They formed a society called the Committee of the Rural Police Association, whose object was to protect the lives and the property of those living in the designated area. The association agreed to subscribe to a fund from which would be paid the wages of a group of policemen. Their duties were to patrol an area of within 10 miles of the city. At first only a few men had been policing the area but as time went on and the subscriptions grew larger, a Superintendent was needed to be in charge of the increasing number of officers. It was reported that Maddison had been appointed to this very responsible post due to the excellent references which he had brought to the interview. When he started work, he was informed that it would be part of his job to collect the subscriptions from the several parties who lived in and around York. He was instructed to pay the subscriptions into the bank on a monthly basis. When he complained that he wasn't paid enough, the committee gave him an extra £10 and agreed that he could keep 5 per cent of all the money collected. He was also responsible for paying the wages of the policemen under him, which amounted to £60 or £70 a month. It had been agreed that this would be paid over to him by Mr George Swann Esq., the bank manager appointed by the association. At first the system worked quite well, but it began to falter around the end of January 1844. During this time, it was reported, 'Since that time no subscriptions had been paid into the bank.'

On 6 July 1844, as arranged, Maddison went to the bank as usual and asked Mr Swann for the men's wages. The bank manager refused to pay him, stating that he had not received anything from him since January and he was 'already out of pocket by the payments'. The matter was brought to the attention of the police and Maddison was arrested and taken to the York Castle Gaol on 17 August 1844. The Governor made a note in his diary for that day, saying that he had:

> ... received one male prisoner for trial. This man has been a Superintendent of Police and seems much cast down. I have put three men to sleep with him in a four bedded cell.

The case was heard before a very crowded courtroom at the York Assizes on 12 December 1844, as the case had attracted so much attention. Maddison was accused of stealing the subscriptions which was the property of Mr George Swann. The jury heard that the prisoner had sent a letter to the solicitor of the Police Force, Mr R.H. Anderson Esq. admitting the offence and asking for leniency. His defence implied that he had no intention of stealing the money, but it was due to his carelessness in paying in the subscriptions. Several witnesses appeared to give a good character to Maddison but it seems that even the jury thought the case was an unusual one. After retiring for three hours, the foreman of the jury stated that they had found the prisoner guilty but with a strong recommendation to mercy. The sentencing was deferred to the next day when the judge, Mr Justice Coleridge, sentenced him to eighteen months' imprisonment with hard labour. The judge told him that he would have most certainly sentenced him to transportation if the records of the Rural Police Association had not also been so carelessly kept. There is little doubt that Maddison would have suffered whilst in prison due to his role, and probably would have to be kept separate from the other prisoners because of it.

Another most curious case of stealing was heard by the judge at the York Assizes on 9 March 1858, when three men were brought in front of him charged with stealing £5. On the 19 December there was a lot of discontent at Middlesbrough (ER), due to the hundreds of men being thrown out of work. Out of sheer desperation, a mob of between 400 and 500 unemployed men had collected in the middle of the town armed with bludgeons and other implements. Angry at the sight of food and provisions being displayed in the shops, the mob decided that they would enter the shops and demanded money or food from shopkeepers of the town. John Flinn, (30), Thomas Campbell (21), Patrick Cornwall (26), and Thomas Hewitt (23) went into a shop and demanded aid from the proprietor, Thomas Brentnall. The shopkeeper felt extremely intimidated at the group of four's demands, and, in an attempt to get rid of them, he gave them £5. Later, after he and several other shopkeepers complained about the intimidation, the four men were arrested. When they appeared at the Assizes, Hewitt stated that he was completely innocent and had nothing to do with the threats and intimidation which had been carried out by the other men. His companions confirmed this and he was discharged. Flinn told the jury in his defence that the men were desperate and that 'want alone had compelled them to solicit alms'. He stated that they had not been aggressive towards Mr Brentnall and that several people had given money voluntarily. The jury found all three guilty but, due to the desperate plight of the men, asked the judge for a recommendation to mercy. The judge agreed and sentenced the men to one month's prison each.

As we have seen, most stealing crimes were usually opportunist, but one daring thief had the nerve to enter Wortley Hall and steal items belonging to a guest of Lord Wharncliffe. On 2 August 1859, Major Frazer was staying at the house at Tankersley near Barnsley (WR). When he retired to bed around midnight, he decided to leave the window open of his ground-floor bedroom as it was a very warm night. In the morning, he found that a thief had crept into the room while he slept and stolen several items. He reported that he had lost a £20 bank note, a pair of boots, a gold pin, two pairs of trousers and a button hook. The police were called and soon identified a man named Joseph Worrall (24), who had been seen in a field close to the Hall at 4 a.m. in the morning. Witnesses had seen the man who was described as having a pair of trousers over his arm. The man, showing little cunning, was next seen at the Black Swan on Snig Hill at Sheffield, where he tried to pay for his breakfast

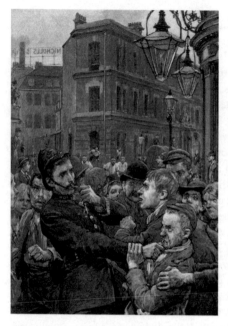

A police constable having to deal with an unruly mob. (*Illustrated London News*)

with a £20 note. The police were called and when he was arrested they found him to be wearing a pair of patent leather boots and a gold pin, which were later identified by Major Frazer to be his stolen property. Worrall appeared at the York Assizes on Wednesday, 7 December 1859 where he was undefended. The judge summed up the case for the jury, who found the prisoner guilty, and he was sentenced to serve twelve months' imprisonment in the Wakefield House of Correction.

Stealing letters from the post office was seen as a case of base actions by an employee and resulted in the post office officials demanding the maximum sentence to be given. Thomas Fisher (22) was brought to the Leeds Assizes on Wednesday, 5 August 1874, charged with stealing a letter containing a gold pendant on 22 May. He was further charged for stealing another letter containing twenty-four penny postage stamps and a half sovereign on the same day. The letters were judged to be the property of the Postmaster General of Leeds (WR). The case against the prisoner was already proven when the prosecution told the judge that there were eighty-five cases of theft already against the prisoner. He told the court that when the prisoner had been arrested, no less than 200 letters, had been found in a cupboard at his lodgings. The judge asked his defence, Mr Wheelhouse, if there was anything to account for stealing the letters to which he admitted that there was no cause. Mr Wheelhouse told his Lordship that he proposed to bring two character witnesses to speak for Fisher but the judge told him that the evidence against him was so clear that it would be of little use. He explained, 'No doubt he had a good character or he would not have been employed by the post office.' The judge sentenced him to five years' penal servitude, stating that he hoped that when he regained his liberty he would strive to regain his former good character. No doubt the judge regretted his comments about the good character of post office employees when the next case was also that of a man stealing letters from the Postmaster General of Dewsbury (WR). Arthur Start had only been employed a few months as an auxiliary letter carrier when he left the service. A few months later, circumstances led to his lodging being searched and letters were found that should have been delivered in February, March and the beginning of April 1874. He was charged with stealing letters containing a cheque for £32 4s 4d, a letter and a post office order for 9s 7d on 10 April 1874. The judge told him:

> You have perhaps given way to some wicked temptation and so got involved in a course of crime. But I should not be doing my duty to the post office and to society at large if I did not sentence you to exemplary punishment.

Ordering him to be imprisoned for five years, the prisoner was led away no doubt reflecting on his crime. Almost certainly, many of these crimes were committed out of sheer desperation and it is probable that many of them were done on the spur of the moment. It is hard for us in our affluent age to understand the sheer poverty that a lot of families went through during these years. However, Assizes judges did not take this into consideration when sentencing these thieves.

Chapter Five

Arson and Explosions

From very early years, the crime of arson was seen as a capital offence committed against a person's property, and the only sentence was that of death. By 1844, the punishment of arson had been reduced for the majority of cases. However, the Assizes judges had the power to impose the maximum sentence where required.

On the night of 1 October 1844, William Potter (30), and his brother in law Thomas went for a moonlight stroll at Whistow, near Selby (NR). The family was aware that Thomas was known to be a weak man and that Potter exerted a strong influence over him. What happened that night was left unclear by the conflicting reports made by the two men. Thomas stated that they walked over the fields to the house of a man called Mr Dixon Potter, where Potter urged him to set fire to some barns. They then went to the house of William Neville, and when they arrived there they found the house was in darkness. Potter once again used many threats to urge Thomas to set fire to the house, which contained Mr and Mrs Neville, several children and her aged father. As the two men ran away back across the fields, they heard shouts of 'fire' and saw the house was ablaze. Thankfully, all the members of the family had escaped. Both men went their separate ways and Thomas went to bed. Potter also went home but it was reported that after only half an hour, he couldn't resist going back to the house to watch 'as a spectator of the mischief of his own hands'. The following morning, Thomas, no doubt regretting his actions of the night before, made a statement to the constable and Potter was arrested. In his conflicting statement, Potter told him that the previous evening he had stopped at a public house where he had two glasses of peppermint. When he left the public house, he met his brother-in-law who asked him to go for a walk with him. They went as far as Mr Dixon's house where Thomas went through the hedge and disappeared. He later returned with 'a light' which he threw away and they ran off. Potter caught up with him in some fields, but before he could stop him Thomas had already set fire to William Neville's house. He was asked why his brother-in-law should make up such lies against him and he told the constable that his wife's family were all against him and had induced Thomas to make the statement, in which he named Potter as the perpetrator. He was arrested and sent to the Assizes to take his trial for arson.

On Wednesday 4 December, he appeared at the Assizes and Thomas once again gave evidence against him. The prosecutor, Mr Wilkins, stated that the fire at Mr Dixon's farm had resulted in the destruction of two hay stacks, a barn, a stable and two horses. The reason Potter gave was that he was a bricklayer and had destroyed the property in the hope that he would be employed to rebuild them. After the fire he had gone to both Dixon and Neville to ask for the job, but both had declined his offer. The judge made a speech in which it was reported that 'his voice indicated the most profound emotion'. He told Potter:

I have considered with the greatest care and I have striven in vain to find any circumstances in the case itself or in your conduct...from abstaining to allow the law to take its course. But when consideration is given to setting fire to a dwelling house with several human beings in it then that exception for everyone to see the propriety of imposing upon that offence the capital punishment.

It was reported that 'his Lordship's voice which could barely be heard' then imposed the death sentence on William Potter, exhorting him, 'Consider your life as drawing to a close and throw yourself on the mercy of him that has no limit.' Potter remained unmoved whilst he was standing in the dock and whilst the sentence was being read out. The Governor of the prison noted in his diary on 25 December 1844 that 'William Potter received a reprieve'. No doubt this was due to his very young age. Instead he found himself transported for life on the ship *David Malcolm*, on 13 May 1845, to Van Diemen's Land.

A later case of arson was heard at the Assizes on 17 March 1860 when the man charged with the offence stated his complete innocence. The man, Thomas Langstaff (35), was charged with setting fire to a stack of hay on the night of 25 May 1859 at Grimesthorpe (WR). A witness saw a man running away from the fire but he was unable to identify him. Only later when Langstaff was in the Sheffield Workhouse did he confess that he had set fire to the stack but that it was a complete accident. As a result of this confession, he was arrested on 7 December 1860 and on his way to the police cells at Sheffield Town Hall, he told the arresting constable that he had been lighting his pipe when a spark started the fire. He was tried by the magistrates and he confessed that he was afraid that he would be charged with starting the fire and, as a consequence of this, he had run away. The magistrate's jury found him guilty despite his protests and he was sent for trial at the Assizes. When Langstaff appeared before the judge, he once again protested his innocence. The judge, in his summing up, directed the jury to acquit the man of any charges; he was of the opinion that there was no case to answer and Langstaff was dismissed, no doubt to his great relief.

Generally speaking, the reasons for setting fire to haystacks were one of revenge. At the Winter Assizes later the same year, two men were charged with arson at Cantley near Doncaster (WR). Francis Henshaw and John Stocks were charged with setting fire to a haystack the property of Samuel Waterhouse of Cantley on the 18 December 1860. It seems that Henshaw had been dismissed by Waterhouse a few days before the fire and had argued with the farmer about the amount of wages he had received. He felt that Waterhouse had kept some of his money back which had been owed to him. In revenge, at about 10.45 p.m., Waterhouse

Sheffield Workhouse. (Courtesy of Picture Sheffield)

noticed that his stack, containing a ton and a half of straw, was on fire. Despite the efforts of some of his neighbours, the stack was completely destroyed. The police were called and made enquiries, where a witness spoke about two men being seen in the field near to the stack at 10 p.m. on the night in question. He identified one of them as Henshaw. Stocks was also interviewed and he stated that he had tried to set fire to the straw but was unable to light his matches. Henshaw then took some matches out of his pocket and proceeded to set fire to the stack. The judge summed up the case for the prosecution and they returned a verdict of guilty for both men. In the sentencing, there is little doubt that Stocks' evidence had gone in his favour, and he was given a lighter sentence of eight months' penal servitude whilst Henshaw was given eighteen months. Both men were to serve their sentence at Wakefield Prison.

It is a well known fact that many young children like to play with fire, but it is seldom that they are taken to the Leeds Assizes charged with setting fire to a stack of hay. On Saturday, 16 December 1865, two boys, George Pool (8) and Matthew Mounsey (8), appeared at the Assizes before Mr Justice Shee.

At 10 a.m. on the morning of 11 November 1864, the two boys were walking a cow down a lane at Bilton (ER) when they passed a labourer named Walker. Both boys were carrying a wisp of straw each, and, when Walker asked what they were doing with the straw, Poole said, 'We are going to set something on fire.' Walker, later that same morning, noticed that there was a stack on fire at the Water Lodge Farm belonging to Mr Wilson. A constable was called and went to Bilton and arrested the two boys, who had just returned home. On the way to the 'lock up', Poole told him that he wanted to make a clean breast of it and informed him that he had held his coat up to shield the matches from the wind, but that Mounsey had been the one to set the stack on fire. Once the fire had started, the boys had become frightened and wanted to try to stamp it out, but they were unable to. Mounsey, when questioned later, denied this and said that Poole had been the one to set fire to the stack. The judge told the court that, from a legal stand point, young people between the ages of seven and fourteen are judged not capable of committing a crime but increasingly he was finding young people below the age of fourteen before him. He told the jury:

> But now you have here these two little boys who seem to have gone very deliberately and got wisps of straw, and stated their intention of setting something on fire. It is to be regretted that we should have to try such children but it is very much regretted that such children should set fire to hay stacks. It is out of the question to pass any but a light sentence on such children.

The jury returned a verdict of guilty on the two boys. The judge told them clearly that if they had been older there is no doubt they would have been given a much harsher sentence. He had spoken to the clergy of the parish where they lived; because both their parents were deemed to be respectable citizens of the community, he ordered that the boys be kept in Leeds Armley Prison for one week, until the end of the Assizes and then they could go home to their parents. He told the boys that they would be better in their care rather than in a reformatory. This compassionate judge, in giving this lenient sentence, no doubt saved the boys from having to mix with more hardened young criminals in the reform school and it is to be hoped that they learned their lesson.

The crime of arson, as we have seen, is usually committed against property rather than people, but when trade union disputes broke out in the Sheffield area during the 1860s, explosive devices were used as bombs. These attacks, which became known as the Sheffield Outrages, were so bad that the militia had been called out to help with the mob. Both the following two cases concerned a type of bomb made from putting gunpowder into a tin can and adding a fuse; both had very astonishing verdicts at the York Assizes.

There was much industrial discontent in Sheffield (WR) in 1861 and trade unions were formed with the intention of protecting their workers. Trouble started when men who had joined the union refused to work with non-union men, and, as a result, reprisals were taken against them and their employers. The trouble started on the night of 21 December 1861 when two explosions were heard at Thorpe Hesley, near Rotherham (WR) around 11 p.m. The explosions were seen to have partially demolished two shops belonging to Charles Butcher and John Hattersley. A witness, Sarah Ann Butcher, swore that she saw three men walking up Kirby Lane leading to the two shops whilst she was talking to her sweetheart. Shortly afterwards, she saw the same three men running past her and identified two of the men as being James Watson and Joseph Tomlinson. After the men had passed her by she then heard an explosion and saw flames coming from the two shops. A search was made of the area but it seems that the three men – Tomlinson, James Watson and his brother Isaac – had gone to Chesterfield. Finally they were arrested at a shop where they were all working and when the premises was searched, identical pieces of tin had been found. The three men were arrested and brought back to Rotherham where they were tried at the West Riding courthouse. A local police officer was called and he gave evidence that he had seen two men, who he identified as Isaac and James Watson, that night at around 9 p.m. on a common at Thorpe. He told the magistrates at the West Riding Courthouse in Rotherham that they told him they had come from Nottingham and asked the way to Barnsley. He pointed in

Rioting and the use of the militia. (*Illustrated London News*)

the direction and the two men conversed in a language which he thought was Welsh. He watched them walk down the road until they reached Senior's public house, where he saw them enter. Shortly afterwards, he heard about the explosion and went to inspect the debris at the two shops. Searching through the remains at Hattersley's shop, he found some tin which corresponded with some he had found at Butcher's shop, which he gave to Sergeant Chinhall of Rotherham police. When Sarah Ann Butcher gave evidence, she told the jury that she had seen Joseph Tomlinson at a union meeting at Thorpe the previous October, where he had been trying unsuccessfully to get people to join the nail-makers union. He left the meeting in disgust, stating to others, 'Come on, that will do. We will blow every bugger up.' A witness said that James Watson had tried to get some of the men working for another local employer to go on strike but when they refused, he told them that it would be the worse for them. The men were

West Riding Courthouse, Rotherham. (Rotherham Archives and Local Studies)

found guilty of throwing gunpowder into the two shops and sent to take their trial at York.

The men appeared before the judge and jury on Tuesday, 18 March 1862 and they seemed confident that they would be freed. The defence, Mr Price QC, criticised the Superintendent of Rotherham police for the fact that he had flattened the pieces of tin found at Chesterfield in order to establish that, along with the two pieces of tin found in the ruined shops they were all the same size. He also questioned the reasons why the men were not immediately arrested after the testimony of Mary Ann Butcher had been given to the Rotherham police. He brought forward witnesses who had been in the public house that night, who stated categorically than none of the prisoners were there but that, at around 9 p.m., two strangers had gone into the pub and were heard to be speaking in Welsh. Crucially, three officers from Chesterfield police all gave evidence that on the night in question, Tomlinson had been seen by all of them in a very drunken state in the company of his wife at Chesterfield.

A woman witness, also from the same town, stated that she had seen Thomlinson and Isaac Watson later that evening heading towards Tomlinson's home. At this point, the learned judge indicated to the prosecution that they should dismiss the prisoners and bring the trial to a close, but when the jury were consulted they gave their unanimous decision that the case continue. A further witness said that James Watson was her next door neighbour and she had seen him on the night in question on two occasions at Belper in Derbyshire. A butcher at Belper said that James Watson had gone to his stall in the market to pick up some meat which had been ordered the week before, and two other witnesses corroborated his story. Four witnesses from Thorpe stated that they had been in the vicinity of Hattersley's shop sooner after the explosion and had heard Sarah Ann Butcher state that she had seen three men in the lane but that she hadn't recognised any of them. The judge summed up the case for the jury, telling them that they must decide who was telling the truth. Was it the Chesterfield police men who had seen Thomlinson by the light of gas lamps, or should they believe Sarah Ann Butcher who had seen the men in a dark unlit lane?' He stated that:

> I am confident their verdict will be founded upon just grounds and that they will come to the right conclusion… the evidence for the defence is that person who had every opportunity of seeing the prisoners and conversing with them; then the jury must wholly accept or wholly reject their testimony. If the jury does not believe them either the witnesses were perjured or mistaken the events of some day for another.

The jury then went to discuss the case, taking the three pieces of tin with them. The court was crowded and it was the opinion of the majority that the men should be acquitted, so it was to complete silence that the jury found all the men guilty when they returned after only forty minutes. The judge accepted the decision of the jury and sentenced the men to fourteen years' imprisonment. It was reported that the faces of Thomlinson and the two Watson brothers showed their bewilderment as they were led from the dock. From this distance in time it does seem that the case and the evidence were handled to the detriment of the Rotherham police. Could the men have been not guilty and sentenced unjustly? We shall never know. In cases like this, that came out of civil disturbance, great pressure was put on police forces to solve crimes, and the actions of the police superintendent in flattening the pieces of tin would not be allowed today. But the unrest about the use of non-union labour had quickly spread to the nearby town of Sheffield. At the same Assizes where Thomlinson and Isaac and James Watson were tried, the following day the jury heard another case of an explosion, which resulted in the death of a completely innocent woman.

In November of 1861, Bridget (or Bedelia) O'Rourke was a lodger at the house of Mr and Mrs Wastnidge of 24 Acorn Street, Sheffield. She was described as 'a fanciful woman who believed in ghosts and such things' and she had only lived at the house a fortnight. O'Rouke had been allocated the front bedroom over the front door of the house. She was not used to having a bedroom to herself and as a consequence had trouble sleeping at night. On 23 November 1861, at sometime between 12 and 1 a.m., a parcel wrapped up in brown paper was flung through her bedroom window. She saw the parcel on the floor, and, picking it up, shouted for her landlord who was asleep in the attic. His wife, who had been awakened by the breaking glass, went to attic window and opened it. She saw two men running away from the house. One of the men, in his haste, caught his coat on some metal projecting into the street; as he turned to free himself she saw his face and recognised him as Joseph Thompson who had worked with her husband.

Mr Wastnidge ran downstairs to where his lodger stood holding a parcel which looked like a can wrapped in brown paper. He noticed that the parcel had sparks coming from it. He shouted at her to throw it away but before she could, the homemade bomb exploded, throwing him backwards and setting the clothes of both O'Rourke and his wife on fire. In a panic, Mr and Mrs Wastnidge went back upstairs to the attic where they both managed to escape by a ladder which had been brought by some neighbours. Meanwhile Bridget had run into the cellar where she was later rescued, although she was in a very badly burned condition. Both women were taken to the infirmary. Mrs Wastnidge was thought at that time to be the most severely injured of the two women, but before long it became clear that O'Rourke was dying and would not live much longer. She made a statement about the night the bomb came through her window to Mr

Wilson Overend, a magistrate for the West Riding. The death-bed statement was also heard and witnessed by Thompson and his solicitor.

Police enquiries established that both Wastnidge and Thompson had worked for a Mr Hoole, who was a fender manufacturer in Sheffield. There had been some dispute in June 1861, and, as a result, Mr Hoole had sacked a number of men, replacing them with non-union workforce. Much agitation was felt about this in the town and meetings were held where reprisals against these non-union men (who were christened 'knobsticks') were discussed. Mr Wastnidge was one of the non-union men employed by Mr Hoole and he and some of the other men had been offered £5 to down tools and walk out. However, after some consultation, they decided that was not enough, but they would consider taking such action for £20 each. Wastnidge told the police he was aware that Thompson had followed him home one night and, as a consequence, he knew where he lived. He told the jury that he had been threatened by Thompson and other men on several occasions. Mrs Wastnidge told the court that she had seen Thompson and another man talking outside a grocer's shop and, as she passed, he had looked at her 'viciously', stating to his companion, 'It will be done.'

At the trial, the chief constable gave evidence stating that when Thompson had been arrested and his house searched, a can similar to the one used in the murder was found. He also had a coat which was torn on the right side, and when he was arrested he appeared to be rather drunk and had used very bad language to his wife. Thompson was sent to the Assizes to take his trial and he appeared there on 19 March 1862. Mr Twibell, a grocer of Snig Hill, gave evidence that the prisoner had, a few days before the explosion, visited his shop for 2lbs of blasting powder. Another shopkeeper, a Mr Henry Wild, a gun maker of High Street, Sheffield, told the jury that they day before the explosion, Thompson had gone to his shop asking if they kept fuses, but was told that they did not. He then went to Mr John Wilson, a hairdresser and dealer in fireworks, and there obtained a fuse. All the three witnesses picked out Thompson in an identity parade. Other men who worked with the prisoner at Messrs

Chamber brewery swore that at the time he was supposedly buying blasting powder and fuses, that he was at work with them. The judge summed up for the jury and he told them:

> It is impossible to disguise from ourselves that there is a state of society that exists in Sheffield which is most prejudicial to the welfare of the town. It is a tyranny of the most fierce and most grinding description which is the duty of every right thinking man to endeavour by all lawful means to put a stop to...There is even a surgeon – an educated man by profession and position – who should be so alarmed at the consequences of giving evidence as to undergo the probability of a commitment to prison rather than be examined as a witness.

There was no evidence suggesting who this seemingly reluctant witness was, but the summing up lasted for two hours. At the end, the jury was dismissed and the court proceeded with another case. After an absence of an hour and a quarter, the judge was told that the jury were now prepared to give their verdict on the explosion case and Thompson was brought back into the court. The court was completely silent as the foreman of the jury gave a not guilty verdict; the court erupted immediately into an uproar. Thompson, clearly delighted, threw his cap in the air before leaving the dock. It was reported that he was seen shaking hands with the prisoners whose trial had been interrupted, and that after the prisoner had left the courtroom 'the jury had a very stormy discussion'.

Chapter Six

Child Murder

Some of the saddest crimes against children were those committed by mothers guilty of killing their illegitimate children. The act of an unmarried woman giving birth to a child vilified her in the eyes of society – the birth was the result of her lack of virtue. Little responsibility was laid at the man's door – it was mostly the woman that was seen to be at fault. At inquests into the deaths of the infants, the coroner tried to establish whether or not the child had led a separate existence from the mother (this was deemed as the child having air in the lungs and taking a breath autonomously, therefore not born dead). The Calendar of Felons of 8 March 1800 records early cases of child murder, which received the harshest sentences that could be imposed.

An entry shows that Mary Thorpe from Ecclesfield (WR) was charged that, on 10 November 1799, she was delivered of a bastard child. Mary was a single woman (21) who had worked as a domestic servant in Sheffield. It was claimed that, in terror, a week after the child had been born, she tied a stone to its neck and cast it into the river where it drowned. She was caught and interrogated, and swiftly sent to York Assizes where she tried to make a case that she was suffering from 'milk fever' at the time. Nevertheless, she was found guilty on the 8 March and it was reported in the Governor's Journal that she 'manifested the most sincere contrition for the-crime of which she had been found guilty'.

Mary was hung the following Monday 17 March and her body also was 'sent for dissection and anatomised'. Another domestic servant, Martha Chapel, was slightly luckier. She was tried at York Assizes on 23 July 1803 with the murder of a female child in Ackworth near Pontefract (WR). Martha (19) was described as 'a fine looking young woman' who had been tried on 15 June by a coroner's jury and found guilty of wilful murder of her child. She was sentenced to be hanged on Monday 1 August, but thankfully her sentence was converted to life imprisonment.

On Saturday, 19 March 1831, a young girl, Ester Dyson, was brought to the York Assizes charged with wilful murder after giving birth to a newly born female child at Ecclesfield (WR) in October 1830. The prisoner (26) was deaf and mute but, with the help of an interpreter, managed to tell the jury that she was innocent. Nevertheless, throughout the trial it was obvious to the court that she was insane and incapable of understanding what was happening to her. Thankfully, the jury recommended that she be kept in custody until Her Majesty's pleasure be known.

Ester Dyson was rather luckier than Mary Durkin of Manningham, near Bradford (WR), who attempted to strangle and secretly bury her newly born female child. She was brought to the Assizes on 4 March 1837, where she was given a judgment of death, which was later commuted to transportation for life. Mary was one of 170 convicts on the *Henry Wellesley*, which left England for New South Wales on 17 July 1837.

By the late 1850s, local magistrates were reducing the crime of child murder by their own mothers to one of 'concealing the birth', which received a much lighter sentence. On Thursday, 18 August 1864, a case was heard of Mary Rhodes of Wakefield (WR), a married woman who had been separated from her husband for fifteen months. No doubt the stigma of giving birth to an illegitimate female child was not lessoned by having a wedding ring on her finger. She was charged with having, on the 5 August, 'feloniously killed and slain her newborn child'. The murder may have been committed as Mary had a job working as a cook at the house of a Mrs Scott and she feared that she would lose her position if the truth emerged. As was usual in these cases,

JAMES MILNES, Efquire, High-Sheriff.

MARY Thorpe,	—	— Guilty, Murder, to be *hanged* on Monday the 17th Day of March, inftant and her Body to be afterwards diffected and anatomized.
Michael Simpfon,	—	— Guilty, Murder, to be *hanged* on Monday the 17th Day of March, inftant and his Body to be afterwards diffected and anatomized.
Sarah Bailey,	—	Guilty, Forgery, *To be hanged.*
John Mac Williams,	—	Guilty, Forgery, *To be hanged.*
Luke Lee,	—	Guilty, Forgery.
William Dalrymple,	—	Guilty, Grand Larceny without the Benefit of the Statute, *To be hanged.*
William Sneed,	—	Guilty, Grand Larceny without the Benefit of the Statute.
Miles Barraclough,	—	Guilty, Horfe Stealing.
John Watfon,	—	Guilty, Horfe Stealing.
George Robinfon,	—	Guilty, Horfe Stealing.
Henry Hirft,	—	Guilty, Sheep Stealing.
Jofeph Walker,	—	Guilty, Sheep Stealing.
Richard Booth,	—	Guilty at the laft Affizes, held for the faid County, of feloniously utte a Counterfeit Half Crown, having been before convicted of being a upon utterer of falfe Money, and Judgment refpited, from Time to until the prefent Affizes.

Calendar of Felons from 1800, which records the death sentence of Mary Thorpe. (Courtesy of City of York Council Archives and Local History)

there had been some suspicion that she had been pregnant, but Mary denied it. She gave birth to the child, who she claimed had been born dead. In this instant, the cause of death could not be determined and the surgeon stated that it was impossible to decide whether the child had led a separate existence from the mother. The Assizes jury gave her the benefit of the doubt and the judge directed them that, as a consequence of the prisoners 'gross negligence', they had no option but to return a verdict of not guilty and the prisoner was discharged. Described as being 'a middle aged woman of a respectable looking appearance', there would have been no doubt that she was very grateful as she left the courtroom. The following day, another case of child murder was heard at the same Assizes. In this instance a woman named Mary Ann Winterbottom (24), another domestic servant, was charged with feloniously attempting to murder her male child, whose body was found in the soil of a privy. The offence had been committed at the prisoner's mother's house at Hunslet near Leeds (WR) and it was whilst she was visiting her mother that she gave birth and attempted to suffocate the child.

The prisoner was employed at a Temperance Hotel in Leeds run by a Mrs Hall and, once again, would not have been able to continue with her employment if the child had lived. Thankfully her defence stated that the murder was committed after she had suddenly been taken into labour and 'as such she was therefore not responsible for her actions'. The jury agreed and found her not guilty; she too was discharged.

A very sad case was heard at York Assizes on Friday, 17 July 1840 of the murder of a child called Hannah Norton, the illegitimate child of Jane Gowland at Acomb near York (NR) on 20 December 1839. The child had been abandoned a few months earlier and placed in the workhouse, where it had been cared for by the workhouse authorities. In December it was rumoured that the mother of the child (21) had since married and the guardians instructed the workhouse supervisor to return the child back to its mother. The overseer complied with the request, and, although Gowland made it quite clear that she did not want the child, Hannah was left with her mother. It was reported that Gowland was alone in the house when the supervisor left the child with her – but neighbours reported that no child had ever been seen by them.

As time passed, the couple left the house and in May new tenants moved in. To their absolute horror, the putrefying body of a female child was found in the coal cellar. The clothes the child wore were the same as she had on 20 December when she was left by the overseer. It was also noted that a piece of cloth had been tied tightly around the neck of the infant. Gowland was arrested and charged with wilful murder and ordered for trial at York Assizes, where she appeared in July 1840. A neighbour gave evidence that Gowland had told her that her new husband had threatened to leave her if she kept the child. The defence implied that under the circumstances, the husband may have been guilty of the crime and she would merely be guilty of aiding and abetting him. He pointed out, as mitigating evidence, that the neighbours had often reported her to be found 'crying bitterly' and it seemed that if she was guilty of the act that she was sincerely repentant. The judge summed up the evidence for the jury and, after being away for an hour, they found her not guilty and she was discharged.

Another much more mercenary case concerning, on this occasion, a villainous father who killed his child, was heard by the York Assizes on 19 April 1846. The child was named Mary (21 months), who had been murdered in order for the father to claim 50s (£2.50 in today's money) in insurance on the child's life. Mary was the eldest of the family of John Rodda (33) of Skipton

(NR), who was a hawker by trade (as were many Irishmen of that time). On Thursday 16 April, the child was taken ill and, thinking that it was having problems through teething, the surgeon recommended a mixture of 2 grains of antimonial powder and 1 grain of calomel. The child continued to be poorly although she rallied a little on Sunday 19 April, enough to take some porridge at around 6 p.m. Just an hour later, however, it was clear that the child was dying. The surgeon was sent for once again; upon his arrival, he found the child lying in its mother's lap, vomiting a dark substance from its mouth. The pinafore which the child was wearing was covered with holes in the material. He gave the child some magnesium and the vomiting ceased. The surgeon called back later again the same evening and once more gave the child some magnesium. Despite his best efforts, the child sadly died at 9 p.m. The surgeon gave information to the police, and Rodda was arrested and charged with murder. It seems that on the evening before the child died, Rodda had bought some oil of vitriol from a druggists shop at Skipton. An inquest was held and he was charged with murder.

On Friday 17 June, he appeared at York Assizes and the prosecution informed the jury that there were just two people present when the child was poisoned. He stated that he was not putting Mrs Rodda on the stand and urged them not to infer anything from this other than the law that a wife could not testify against her husband and vice versa. A witness claimed that Rodda had said to him that if the child died he would get 50s from 'a dead club' and that 'the sooner it was dead the better as it was so sickly'. The jury, after having hearing all the evidence, retired for two hours and returned with a guilty verdict. The judge gave the death sentence, telling Rodda not to entertain any thought of a reprieve. After issuing the sentence, Rodda, who was a Catholic, was served by Revd Bellington, a Roman Catholic priest attached to York Castle Prison, the Catholic Dean of York. At an early hour on Saturday 8 August, workmen erected the scaffold at the front of St George's field, where already people were arriving to witness the execution; whilst he spent his last few hours in the condemned cell. By the appointed time, there were hundreds of people, many of them Irish, on the grass in front of the scaffold. Rodda walked

A condemned cell, York Castle Prison. (Courtesy of York Museum Trust)

onto the scaffold already pinioned; the hangman pulled the cap over his eyes and adjusted the rope; he then pulled the bolt which launched him into eternity. The Governor's diary for York Castle noted, 'John Rodda was buried this evening, four feet from the projection in the wall of the condemned cell in the presence of Mr Watson the Deputy Sheriff, Revd Bellington and myself.'

Little consideration was given in earlier years to the possible resulting psychological impact on a woman who committed child murder. These cases give the impression that women who killed their illegitimate children were to be pitied rather than punished. Thankfully, fathers like John Rodda were few and far between – although it does highlight the dangers of the burial clubs that proliferated during the nineteenth century.

Chapter Seven

Manslaughter

Manslaughter is a term which is used when the intention to kill or 'malice aforethought' cannot be proved. In such cases, a term of imprisonment was recorded and the length of the sentence depended on the severity of the crime. Many of these crimes were committed in 'the heat of the moment' and one of the most common causes for manslaughter was when the people concerned had been drinking. The following case concerned a hairdresser of Vicar Lane, Leeds (WR) who, at 2 a.m., was attacked at a short distance from his shop, which seemingly was still open for business.

The details of the case were described at an inquest on the body of Thomas Stodhart, on the morning of Sunday, 29 March 1840. The coroner was told that two men had been taken into custody by the night watchmen, who were identified as George Oldroyd and Richard Gresty. Stodhart's apprentice of six years, James Addiman gave evidence that the two men had been in the shop at 9 p.m. on Saturday 14 March, and that he had shaved Gresty on that occasion. Two weeks later, they again went into the shop and Gresty told Addiman to take some more off his whiskers as there was more on the left than the right and his workmates had been plaguing him about it. Addiman did as requested, whilst Stodhart left the shop and walked up Vicar Lane. He stated that both men, as well as his master, had been drinking but that none of them were intoxicated. He watched them catch up with his master and then he saw Stodhart and Oldroyd start to wrestle with each other. He ran up and stood between the two men to prevent them fighting, but then Gresty caught his head under his arm and pulled him away to the other side of the street and started to punch him. When he was finally released, Addiman saw the hairdresser still on the floor and the two attackers running away. He shouted for the watch to come; they eventually came and took the seriously injured man to his home. There he was attended by the surgeon, a Mr Garlick, who found several broken ribs on the man's left side, but noted there were little outward signs of violence. He attended him for five days until Friday 2 April, when he died. The surgeon told the jury that, in his opinion, the injuries which caused his death were consistent with someone kneeling on the deceased man as he lay on the ground. The jury took only a few minutes to record a verdict against the two men, finding them guilty of manslaughter, and they were sent to the Assizes to take their trial.

The case was heard on Wednesday, 15 July 1840 and once again the apprentice Addiman gave evidence. He told the judge that he saw the men sparring and had heard the deceased man say to Oldroyd, 'We are both of a size.' His companion Gresty told Oldroyd, 'Go at him [George]'. Oldroyd then punched Stodhart so hard he knocked him to the ground. He then threw himself upon him. He continued punching the man, who by now was shouting out 'murder'. His wife saw from the shop what was happening and she also called out for the watch. The jury heard all the evidence and retired for an hour and a half before finding Gresty not guilty and Oldroyd guilty of manslaughter. The judge sentenced Oldroyd to be imprisoned for three months in York Castle Prison. As a prisoner in York Castle, Oldroyd would find his life very different from the life he had led on the streets of Leeds. Prisoners were deprived of meals or given bread and water for any infringement of the rules and the only exercise they had was in Half Moon Yard. Attempts to escape were dealt with very severely. The gaoler's journal for 19 July 1829 records that 'Ten men were put into close confinement for attempting to escape

Half Moon Yard, York Castle Prison. (Courtesy of York Museum Trust)

through the wall of Half Moon Yard and four more were put into irons for the same offence.' Perhaps Oldroyd was lucky that he only had to serve three months.

Another case of manslaughter that occurred under the influence of alcohol, led to a six-month term of imprisonment with hard labour. Mr J.C. Warren was a commercial traveller from Wolverhampton, who, as part of his work, often made the journey to York (NR). On Thursday, 1 April 1841, he was in York once more and stayed, as he usually did, at the White Swan Hotel, Pavement, York. Mr Warren was a man who worked hard and played even harder, so, by 9 p.m., he was found in the Star Inn in Stonegate where he had several drinks with a colleague – one Mr Monkman, a solicitor of his acquaintance. The two men were quite merry by the time they left the pub, which was around 1.30 a.m. When they got to the White Swan, they saw that no one was up and the hotel was locked up for the night. Mr Monkman told Mr Warren that he was welcome to come home with him, where he would be able to find Mr Warren a bed. Mr Warren declined, however, deciding instead to go to a lodging house for the night, belonging to a Mrs Tyne, on St Andrewgate. They had reached Church Street when they noticed two men standing at the other side of the street. One of them, later identified as William Pleasie, shouted abuse at them, telling them to 'Go to hell you two buggars.' Mr Monkman, sensing trouble, told his friend to get away as quickly as possible but Mr Warren's blood was up. Warren tried to placate the man, saying, 'Don't fight my good man', but it was too late and the prisoner grabbed hold of Monkman and the two men began to fight.

Monkman, by now thoroughly frightened, broke away from Pleasie and ran towards King's Square. Pleasie ran after him, shouting all the time that he would kill him if he caught up. Monkman managed to escape and returned to find Warren still struggling to escape from the other unknown man. Pleasie hit Warren so hard that he fell to the pavement with a thud. He then sat astride the poor man and smashed his head repeatedly into the stone floor, creating such a disturbance that people were coming to the window to see what the commotion was. Mr Chapman, who lived opposite, witnessed Pleasie smashing Warren's head repeatedly on the ground. His evidence was corroborated by another neighbour, a Miss Hauxwell. Eventually, the two men, noting that they were now being observed, ran away. Monkman, who also had been hiding, came back to find his friend insensible on the floor. Strangely enough, he did manage to lift him to his feet to get to Mrs Tyne's house. The lodging housekeeper let him in and after washing his hands and face he went to bed, complaining of a pain in his head. The following morning, however, he could not wake up and a surgeon, Mr Abbey, was called to the house. He tried to help the poor man as much as he could, but he lapsed deeper into unconsciousness until 11.30 p.m. the following night when, tragically, he died. Pleasie was arrested and tried in the Guildhall at Leeds on Wednesday, 21 July 1841, although his companion was not identified. Inevitably he was found guilty by the jury, and the judge, Mr Justice Wightman, sentenced to six months with hard labour.

In Halifax (WR), as in many other parts of the country in the nineteenth century, there was much discrimination against Irish people. Subsequently, there developed an Irish Quarter in the town. In December 1844, two Irishmen from the area had a quarrel. As a result, James Tansey was brought to the Assizes in December 1844, accused of having killed Daniel Martin by stabbing him close to his ear. Although no evidence was given regarding the reasons for the row, Martin was observed pursuing Tansey's sister and brandishing a knife along Hatter's Yard in Halifax. She fled into the house of her brother; Martin followed her into the house and struck her on her head and then started to attack Tansey. A scuffle ensued, and, having pushed Martin into a corner, Tansey struck him on the left side of his neck with a knife.

By this point, other witnesses had assembled in the house and were trying to separate the two men. Martin fell to the floor and the blood gushed out of his neck so quickly, having severed a main artery, that it was reported it resembled 'turning on a tap'. In a fit of pique, Tansey pushed the dying man out of the house. However, witnesses told the court that he, once again, went outside to where Martin was now unconscious. He made more threats and stated that if he hadn't killed him already, he would make sure that he was dead. A constable was called and Tansey was arrested; Martin was taken to the infirmary where he unfortunately died the following morning. The defence pointed out that the prisoner was now sorry for his actions, which he claimed were carried out in the heat of the moment. He also asked the jury to take into consideration the level of provocation Tansey had received from Martin in his own house. The jury retired for only a few minutes, then returned back to the court and delivered a verdict of guilty, although they recommended mercy on account on the provocation to the deed. The judge agreed and sentenced Tansey to six months' imprisonment with hard labour.

What should have been a happy occasion led to a man counting himself lucky to get away with the crime of manslaughter at Horton, near Bradford (WR) in 1859. The judge who heard the case described it as being 'little short of murder'. Thomas Clarke was celebrating a christening at his house with relatives and friends, which resulted in them drinking for most of the day. One of those invited to the christening was a man called Patrick Coley, who offered to go and to get some more alcohol. Mr and Mrs Clarke had by this point had enough, and wanted to go to bed. They had repeatedly asked Coley to go home but the offer was, each time, repudiated, even though most of the houseguests had already left. Coley predictably turned nasty, and he aggressively challenged Clarke to throw him out of the house. Clarke complied, and the door was swiftly locked against him. Annoyed at the attitude of his friend, Coley started kicking on the door until Clarke was forced to open it again, whereupon he brutally stabbed him three times in the stomach. The stab wounds were so deep that part of his bowel was exposed. The police were called and Coley was quickly arrested. When he was brought to the York Assizes on Tuesday 6 December, the judge told him:

> The jury have found you guilty of manslaughter upon evidence which must have satisfied them and all who have heard your case feel that this is one of the worst species of the crime of which you have been found guilty.

He then gave him one of the longest terms of imprisonment that he could on a charge of manslaughter, sentencing him to fifteen years in prison.

On Tuesday, 11 December 1860, the jury at York Assizes heard a case of such inhuman cruelty that the accused was lucky not to have incurred a similar sentence. The court heard how a man named William Walsh (48) had kept his wife imprisoned in a garret of a house at Clifton near Otley (ER), whilst caddishly living with another woman in the lower part of the house. He had forbidden his wife to ever go downstairs, and she lived in fear of him. The neighbours became concerned when they had not seen her for many months, and, in August 1860, they took advantage of his absence to go into the house – where they eventually found her in the garret on a bed. She was in a filthy state – clearly starving and emaciated as she cowered on a dirty mattress. The woman was plainly terrified that her husband would return and find the neighbours there. A constable was called, who made arrangements for the woman to be transferred to York Workhouse, where she sadly died on 21 August. Walsh was arrested and charged with manslaughter and sent to York Assizes to take his trial. He appeared before Mr Justice Hill, who pulled no punches when he addressed the jury. He told them that:

The prisoner has kept his wife in a state of almost complete imprisonment and has deprived her of the common necessities of life, when he was in a position to provide for her. Having formed a relationship with a female, which was inconsistent with his duty to his wife, he began to ill treat her. He kept her in an attic room access to which alone could be reached by a step ladder. Here he kept her without food and in a filthy condition, and his bad treatment caused her death.

He stated that Walsh's cruelty to his wife was one of the worst cases of manslaughter that he had heard and he promptly sentenced Walsh to four years' imprisonment.

The Assizes often heard cases of drunken cruelty inflicted by husbands on their wives, but, on 13 November 1860, the accused was seen as a woman suffering under great provocation. On the night in question, George Johnson returned home, inebriated, to greet his wife, Elizabeth (35), at 11 p.m in their house in Day's Court, Frenchgate, Doncaster (WR). He was a labourer, occasionally employed as a billsticker, and was well known around the town for his regular overindulgence and bad temper. He soon got into an argument with his wife who, seizing a large piece of wood, hit him across the head, inflicting a wound on his forehead about 2ins long. He dropped to the floor and died at 2 a.m. the following morning, having not regained consciousness. Elizabeth was arrested and she told the magistrates court that he had always been a violent man – particularly when he had been drinking. The jury had no option but to find her guilty of manslaughter and to send her for trial at the next Assizes. She took her place in the dock on Tuesday, 11 December 1860 in front of Mr Justice Hill. Her solicitor, Mr Price, informed the court that Johnson had subjected his wife to ill-treatment for many years, and, on the night in question, he came home and physically attacked her once again. In self defence, she claimed she had taken the piece of wood and hit him with it. When the judge asked her if there was anything she wanted to say, she told them that she was sorry for what she had done. The jury returned with a verdict of guilty, but with a recommendation to mercy due to the provocation she had received at her husband's hands. The judge reserved sentencing to

The Minster Church of St George, Doncaster.

the following Thursday, and it was probable that Mrs Johnson left the dock convinced she would have a prison sentence served on her. Incredibly, when she returned back into court two days later, the judge told her that he could not believe that she intended to kill her husband and that he was sure she had acted in a moment of passion. He then declared her not guilty and she was discharged after thanking the court for her liberation.

Many crimes of manslaughter were the result of a quarrel, particularly when combined with alcohol. On 11 June 1874, one Thomas Haigh – a drayman of Mytholmroyd, near Halifax (WR) – got into an argument with William Henry Stansfield. The dispute concerned the right way to turn a horse and cart and had started in the Dusty Miller at Mytholmroyd – a public house – and continued into the White Lion, another public house in the vicinity. The landlord, fearing that a fight would break out, threw the men out of his pub and was not surprised to see that the two had barely got a few yards before they started punching one another. The two men were fighting on the canal bank; Haigh was sitting on top of Stansfield, who was holding Haigh's head. With the help of several others, the two men were separated. But, before Stansfield could get up off the floor, Haigh kicked him in

A view of Halifax, West Riding. (Courtesy of Sue Trickey)

the groin. Stansfield was later taken to the Halifax Hospital where he died the following day. Haigh was arrested and charged with manslaughter and appeared before the magistrate court. He was quickly found guilty and was sentenced to take his trial at Leeds Assizes. He appeared before Mr Baron Amphlett on Tuesday, 11 August 1874. One of the hospital surgeons gave evidence and told the jury that he had held a post-mortem on the body and had found that Stansfield had died from a rupture of the bladder. His Lordship stated to the jury:

> I consider it desirable that it should be known particularly in the North of England where kicking cases are so common that the use of thick boots in kicking is in fact making use of a dangerous weapon.

The jury was then sent out to consider their verdict and apparently thought there was no case to answer. Haigh was found not guilty and discharged.

These cases all point to the impulsiveness behind the crime of manslaughter. Men and women of Yorkshire, particularly during the expanding time of rapid industrialisation, were forced to live in squalor, where the only outlet for their dissatisfaction was through alcohol. Thus, manslaughter was often the unfortunate result of arguments.

Chapter Eight

Poaching

Poaching was a fairly serious crime in the nineteenth century. The issues around it were debated long and hard in the courts and various newspapers of the period. Many of the working men had seen poaching as a right to supplement the meagre food supply available during the winter months. Game Laws were introduced when landowners saw poaching as an infringement of their property. To the poachers, gamekeepers were seen as the enemy protecting the land for the gentry – never bypassing the chance to shoot a rabbit or a couple of pheasants. As more and more laws came into effect, punishments became increasingly severe, which led to friction between the two parties. Magistrates in the Yorkshire area became more concerned when, instead of poachers operating individually, they grouped together in gangs at night and went out heavily armed.

When poachers fell out, quite often the result might have been murder. A curious tale was told at Hutton Rudby (NR) following the sudden disappearance of a local poacher known as William Huntley. Some eleven years passed before his accused murderer was brought to trial. Despite his poaching activities, Huntley was the son of a wealthy farmer and was known to have £85 13s 4d on him when he disappeared in July 1830. On 22 July, he went to visit an old poaching friend, one Robert Goldsborough.

The police were called in when he had been missing for a few days and neighbours were beginning to get concerned. Goldsborough told them that Huntley had stayed with him a day or two before returning home, and, before they parted company, had told him he was planning to go to America. As the police continued their enquiries, it emerged that a witness, one James Maw, stated that he had seen Huntley in the afternoon of the 30 July in the company of Goldsborough and another poaching friend, George Garbutt. They were near to Crathorne Woods and the group had invited him to join them – stating that they were going to shoot a hare and roast it for supper – but Maw refused to go with them. A farmer later reported hearing shots at eleven o'clock that same night coming from the direction of Crathorne Woods.

After Huntley's disappearance, Goldsborough's house was searched by the constable, who found six shirts with the initials 'WH' on them, along with Huntley's watch and some money. Goldsborough told him that Huntley had given him the watch and money to pay off as part of a debt. Huntley's body was never found, and, shortly after this, Goldsborough moved out of the area to live at Barnsley (WR). He found a job as a weaver and changed his name to Robert Towers. The other poacher, Garbutt, had at the same time been involved in the robbery from a barn and he also left the neighbourhood.

In June 1841, some workmen who had been digging ditches found a skull, pelvis and some other, obviously human, bones. An inquest was held on the remains, after which the surgeon deduced that they were male. He stated that the unknown man had died after being hit on the head by a sharp instrument which had fractured the skull and broken the bones of his nose. The coroner summed up the evidence and the jury brought in a verdict that, 'the man had been killed by a person or persons unknown'. Even though it was eleven years later, a local constable PC Garnon remembered the accusations of 1830 and on the 23 June 1841, he took the skull with him to Barnsley in order to confront Goldsborough with the evidence. He put the skull down on the table and asked him if he thought the skull resembled that of Huntley. Goldsborough, visibly shaken, insisted that he knew nothing of it. Meanwhile, another poacher, Thomas Grundy, gave evidence to the magistrates on Friday 12 and Saturday, 13 August 1841. Soon after, warrants had been issued for both Goldsborough and Garbutt. Goldsborough was arrested at Barnsley, but Garbutt was never found. Thomas Grundy told the magistrates that Goldsborough had called him out of bed one night after Huntley had disappeared to go poaching. Goldsborough had been acting very suspiciously, and when they reached Wearybank Wood, he showed him a large parcel and asked Grundy to help him to lift it. Grundy tried, but the parcel was too heavy. When he dropped it onto the ground, to his surprise a head rolled out, which he identified as Huntley's. Goldsborough was visibly agitated – so much so that it took him five minutes before he could regain his composure.

Goldsborough told Grundy that Huntley had been shot accidentally, but Grundy didn't believe him and fled the scene. Goldsborough bellowed after him that if he told anyone, he would kill him. Grundy told the court that he refused to go out at night for as long as Goldsborough remained in Hutton and was very relieved when he knew that he had left the area. Goldsborough was then questioned and he repeated the story about Huntley going to America. Meanwhile, Grundy had taken PC Garnon and Barthram to Wearybank Wood and showed them the place where the body had been laid – but, after such a long period of time, there was no evidence remaining. The jury returned a verdict that both Grundy and Goldsborough were guilty and sent the pair to York Castle Prison to take their trial at the Assizes.

On 18 August 1841, the York Governor Mr Noble recorded in his journal that Thomas Grundy had strangled himself in his cell with a silk handkerchief. He had been found by one of the turnkeys at 5 a.m., hanging from one of the bars of the window, and the body was

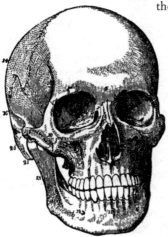

A Skull, similar to that taken from the house of Robert Goldsborough.

reported as being 'still warm'. Several efforts to revive Grundy were made to no avail. An inquest was held and the recorded verdict was that he had 'killed and then murdered himself'. Grundy's body was buried at St Mary's cemetery on Castlegate at 9 a.m. on 29 August 1841. The Assizes took place on Wednesday 9 and Thursday, 10 December 1841, where almost thirty witnesses were called to aid the prosecution. There had been a debate as to whether Grundy's statement, which had been made before he died, could be read out in court. After some consideration, the judges allowed the statement to be read. The following day, the defence of the prisoner was heard. Mr Wilkins questioned the testimony of the deceased, and Grundy pointed out that he might have killed himself in remorse for telling lies about his friend. After a speech, which lasted over three hours, he finally asked the jury to give Goldsborough the benefit of the doubt in this case.

The judge summed up the case for the jury, illustrating the many discrepancies and the jury returned within half an hour with a verdict of not guilty. Goldsborough looked relieved as he finally left the dock. If he did indeed get away with murder, he took that secret with him to the grave.

In revolt against the increasing Game Laws, poachers were carrying guns which they fully intended using against the gamekeepers. To make the situation worse, gamekeepers were also carrying weapons with which to protect themselves. By the middle of the nineteenth century, harsh penalties were handed out to poach-

St Mary's church, Castlegate, York.

ers who had more than one offence against them, resulting in long prison or transportation sentences.

In the next case, when the gamekeepers saw that they were outnumbered with guns, they tried to walk peacefully away, but such was the anger against the unfairness of the Game Laws that two keepers were shot. Lord Hawke employed gamekeepers at Womersly (NR) in woods in that area containing game. At midnight on 21 November 1853, his gamekeeper, John Mitchell, and others heard shooting coming from Birdspring Woods. Along with Mitchell was an under-keeper named Hepworth and five other people. Hepworth and Mitchell carried guns and the five others carried heavy sticks. When the keepers spotted the poachers, they saw that there were five of them and they were carrying two double-barrelled guns and two single-barrelled guns. Facing the men with their weapons drawn, Hepworth shouted, 'Act like men and do not use your guns!' When it became clear that the men were not going to disperse, Mitchell told them, 'We shan't take you, go away like men.' The keepers, knowing they were not as well armed as the poachers, attempted to walk away, but shots were fired, hitting Mitchell and Hepworth. Mitchell was shot in the eyes and Hepworth was also shot, resulting in almost seventy pieces of shot later being removed from his body.

The police were called and the search for the poachers began. A man called George Kemp told the police that on the night of the shooting, William Andrews, Robert Drew and some other men had gone out of the house where he lodged at Doncaster armed with two double-barrelled and two single-barrelled shotguns, as well as an air rifle. Andrews and Drew were arrested and sent to the Assizes. The defence made little of Kemp's statement, telling the jury that he could not be relied upon and that there was little evidence to identify the men who had fired at the gamekeepers. But the most damning point in the trial was when Mitchell was led into the witness box wearing a green shade over his eyes. He told the jury that one of his eyes had been shot out and he had lost the sight of his other eye. He said that he heard the first shot and then as he turned round he was shot in the face. Several witnesses were brought into court to give good characters for the two accused but it was all to no avail, and the jury returned a verdict of guilty for both men.

Drew was found guilty of an attempt to murder, and Andrews with intent to do grievous bodily harm. The judge told Drew that he was passing on him the death sentence but that an application would be made to Her Majesty to have the sentence commuted to transportation for life. Andrews was sentenced to be transported for fifteen years and he sailed out of England on the *Stag*, which left on 2 February 1855, bound for Western Australia. The following year, Drew was transported on the *Runnymede* along with 248 other convicts, to begin life in Western Australia, on 11 June 1856.

Antagonism over previous fines for poaching precipitated the next case, in 1861, which resulted once more in a death sentence being handed down. James Waller was a notorious poacher in Low Springs, near Bingley (NR), and was well known to the game-keepers of the area. William Smith was a gamekeeper employed on the estate of Timothy Hawksworth Esq., a West Riding magistrate residing at Hawksworth Hall. Waller had been a wool comber by trade but had got a reputation as a dangerous poacher after shooting at another gamekeeper by the name of Bradley in August 1860. He had been sentenced to six months' imprisonment for this crime in the Wakefield House of Correction. Following his release he was in court twice in fifteen months, accused by Smith for 'trespassing in pursuit of game', for which he had been fined £2 10s on each occasion. Waller swore to Thomas Inman, a police sergeant at Marston, 'You will never have the chance of taking me to Otley again. Before I will be taken, I will blow his [Smith's] brains out.' Smith was equally determined that he would catch Waller and on the morning of 4 November 1861, he asked another gamekeeper, John Fawcett, to be at Birk's End at 5 a.m. and he would be at Spring's End where he was convinced that Waller would be poaching in the early morning rather than at night. The two places were about 400 yards apart and approximately the same distance from Waller's house.

Both gamekeepers took up their positions and stayed quietly at their post until about 6.30 a.m. when Fawcett heard a single shot coming from Smith's direction. He stayed at his post and heard no more until just before 7 a.m. when he heard another two more shots coming from the direction of Waller's house. He had barely gone 400 yards to where Smith should have been waiting before a man named Joseph Batley shouted that he had found the game-keeper who had been shot. Batley told him that he had heard the shot followed by Smith's voice stating, 'Oh Waller, oh Waller.' Other people heard the shouts and came running to the scene where it appears that the gamekeeper was still alive. Around the body stood Mr Batley senior and three other men named Robinson, Moorhouse and Joseph Greenwood. Mr Batley had sent his young son off to get some assistance. When Greenwood asked Smith, 'What is the matter with you lad?', Smith replied, 'Jim Waller has shot me'. Incredibly, Waller was then seen approaching the wall around the field in his shirt sleeves and when Greenwood asked him, 'Has thou done this?', Waller told him he had not been out of the house all morning. Smith, who was still on the ground, stated, 'It was Waller and no other.' Greenwood called to Waller to come into the field and face Smith, to tell him that he wasn't responsible; Waller refused to go near the body. Greenwood shouted out to him, 'Thou art a villain then and will have to answer for it here or hereafter.' Smith shouted out to him to come and help him, for he claimed to be, a 'done man'. The gamekeeper was lifted to the nearby house of Mr Batley and a surgeon of Baildon, named Steel, came to attend to the stricken man. Steel found him in a state of collapse, with sixty or seventy pellets in his abdomen and chest. The surgeon stayed with his patient until 1 p.m. when he died. Smith had stated several times that he was aware he would not recover, and swore that it was Waller who had shot him. Waller was arrested and sent for his trial at the York Assizes, where he appeared on Wednesday, 18 December 1861. The witnesses were heard but the jury had no option but to find him guilty after deliberating for only three quarters of an hour. Throughout the trial, Waller had remained impassive and showed no signs of remorse for taking the gamekeepers life.

The last days of Waller as a condemned man were described in the *Sheffield and Rotherham Independent*. It seems that prior to committing the crime, he had shown no signs of religious fervour, but since his capture he had become 'extremely penitent'. Waller maintained that – although he was guilty of the crime – he had no intention of taking any life and that only Smith's determination to capture him had driven him to it. On the morning of Friday

The exercise yard at York Castle Prison. (York Museum Trust)

3 January, Waller was visited in his cell by his wife and three children; the meeting was described as being 'agonising'. In the afternoon, he had a meeting with one of his brothers and at 7 p.m. he was attended by the chaplain of York Castle, who stated in his journal that he was 'in a more resigned state than he had been since receiving the death sentence'. From 9 p.m. until 11 p.m., the officers of the prison read the scriptures to him and psalms and hymns were sung at intervals in which he joined in. He retired to bed at 11.10 p.m. and slept until 4.30 a.m. on the morning of his execution.

Crowds of between 10,000 and 12,000 assembled before York Castle to see Waller hung by Thomas Askern of Maltby near Rotherham. At 7 p.m., he was visited by the Deputy Governor Mr Green, and, as they walked in the exercise yard at the Castle Prison, he told Mr Green that he knew he would be in heaven shortly. He had a hearty breakfast at 8 p.m., after which he was visited by the chaplain once more. At 11 a.m., he took the sacraments and seemed to be prepared to meet his doom. Shortly before noon on 4 January 1862, at the time set for the execution, he was visited by the hangman Thomas Askern, who had arrived at York Castle the previous night. He was restrained, and, precisely at the stroke of twelve o'clock, he appeared on the newly erected gallows. Although he walked with a firm step, his face was reported to have been of a 'ghastly hue' – he also appeared so wrapped up in prayers that he seemed to be in a daze. He joined the chaplain in prayer, and, after shaking his hand, had a white cap put over his face and the rope was fastened around his neck. The crown heard him repeat in a loud voice, 'Lord have mercy on my soul.' A newspaper reporter who witnessed the scene reported a 'large moan or groan' was audible from the crown, as 'the bolt was pulled and he was launched into eternity'. Death was instantaneous, although there were muscle spasms for a moment or two. After an hour, the body was cut down and buried near to the condemned man's cell, where he had spent his last moments alive. Before he died, he was said to have stated to the chaplain:

> I have had my revenge and this is my reward but I hope that Smith is in heaven and I trust I shall meet him there soon. There is no bad feeling now.

Throughout the nineteenth century, poaching was dealt with differently by magistrates; not all were in favour of the Game Laws. Sentencing, as we have seen, was down to the judge himself and it was suggested that Waller died on the scaffold because he had the audacity to poach on the land of a magistrate. Nevertheless, his claim that he did not intend to kill Smith was negated by the fact that he had told a police constable that he would not be fined for poaching again. When Waller uttered those words, he did not realise that they would prove to be so prophetic in dictating his own unfortunate demise.

Chapter Nine

Burglary

Burglary was rife throughout the nineteenth century. Sometimes the loot was small, such as pocket watches or clothing, but more lucky burglars could make off with coins, banknotes or even jewellery. For many successful burglars, a property would have to be staked out for many days before the robbery took place, and, as a consequence of this, many of these villains were identified by being seen in the area when they were watching the house.

On the night of 2 March 1840, three men entered the house of a woman farmer, one Mrs Mary Kent of Beckwithshaw, near Harrogate (NR). This robbery was to be the first of several carried out in the North Riding area by the same men. The rapid succession with which they were committed, together with the threats of great violence, threw all the surrounding areas into a state of alarm. The gang consisted of George and Thomas Atkinson, (35 and 33 respectively), John Sanderson (23) and his brother George (24). A significant factor in the burglaries was that the gang always used horrific violence to threaten the occupants, saying they would be killed if they made any noise. At the farm of Mrs Kent, the burglars got away with £42 in gold and silver, a promissory note for £400, a silver watch and a great deal of clothing. Two nights later, the same thieves attacked again, disguised in masks; this time their target was a toll house at Burnt Gate, near

Ripley (NR). A man shouted to the toll keeper to open his door, as a horse and gig were waiting to go through the toll gate. The gang seized the toll keeper as he opened the door, and, using great force, threw him to the ground, breaking his collar bone and cutting his face. One of the robbers held him on the ground whilst the others searched the toll house, stealing £2 in money and a watch.

The men escaped and, later that same night, entered the premises of Mr Shepherd, another farmer living at Killinghall, near Harrogate. The gang again wore masks and had pistols in their hands. Mr Shepherd, on hearing the noise, got out of bed, arming himself with the nearest thing he could (the spoke of a wheel), and stood at the top of the stairs. The men came up the stairs and one put a pistol to his head and the other to his chest, swearing that they would kill him if he resisted. One of the gang stood watching over him, whilst the others searched the house. They found £5 in money, a silver watch, a considerable amount of silver plate, a gold brooch set with diamonds and more clothing. By the time the search had ended, daylight was setting in and the men were anxious to leave and be on their way. Such was their hurry that they left two of the masks and a glove behind in the farmhouse.

The gang might have finished for that night but four days later, they attacked again. On the evening of the 6 March, they broke into a lonely public house at Bushy Strop, near Thirsk (NR), which was kept by a widow named Mrs Anne Kettlewell. Two of the men had blackened their faces and went into the first bedroom, where Mrs Kettlewell's brother was sleeping, and took from him £12 in money. The gang left

A pocket watch, similar to that stolen from Mrs Kent's farm.

him, promising to murder him if he raised the alarm and went to the landlady's bedroom. Pushing the pistols in her face, they swore that they would set fire to the pub with her inside it if she did not show them where the money and valuables were kept, and, fearing for her life, she showed them. They then entered the bedroom of a lodger named Oliver, stealing from him £2 and again threatening to 'blow out his brains'.

The gang then went into the bedroom of a second lodger, named Charles Spence. He had heard the commotion and was out of bed when the tallest of the burglars threatened 'No resistance or your life!' The burglar at that point was carrying a pistol in one hand and a knife in the other. From Spence they took four £5 notes, a promissory note for £100 and some clothing. The burglars then disappeared once again. When the crimes came to the attention of Thomas Ellington, Collinson, the chief officer of police at Boroughbridge and Samuel Winn, the chief officer of the city of Ripon, they were left in no doubt that the same men had committed all the robberies. From information and descriptions received, they identified the men, and a warrant for their arrest was issued. The police were informed that all of the wanted men had gone to London, where George and Thomas Atkinson and John Sanderson were found at a house on Holland Street, Westminster. When the house was searched, they found articles which had been taken from all the four burglaries. The prisoners gave little resistance and from information given to them the police then went to Wellington Barracks where the fourth prisoner, George Sanderson, was apprehended. He was a private in the 3rd battalion of Grenadier Guards and was charged with receiving stolen goods, knowing them to have been stolen. The men were returned back to Ripon to take their trial.

It seems that the four robbers had long been operating in the North and West Riding of Yorkshire. Thomas Atkinson had recently returned from transportation to Botany Bay, where he had served seven years for a burglary committed in Yorkshire in 1833. The men were brought into a crowded courtroom at Ripon on Saturday, 19 April 1840, where there were a total of eleven charges of burglary against them. There were many witnesses who identified them and the judge ordered that they were to be sent to York

A pistol
resembling the one
used by the Yorkshire burglars.

Castle to take their trial. The four men
appeared at the Assizes on Wednesday,
15 July 1840, where Ann Kettlewell told the
court that she identified George Atkinson as she had
seen him 'passing my house frequently'. After hearing all
the evidence, the judge summed up for the jury, who took no
time to find all of the men guilty, and they were sentenced to be
transported for life. The gang was split up for transportation, with
George Atkinson and John Sanderson being on the *Asia V* leaving
from Portsmouth on 12 April 1840, among a total of 260 convicts.
The ship arrived at Van Diemen's Land on 21 August 1841 after a
voyage of 126 days. Thomas Atkinson and George Sanderson were
both transported on the *Lady Raffles* on 2 December 1840 and
they landed in Van Diemen's Land on 17 March 1841.

On Friday, 12 March 1841, William Ibbotson, John Griffin
and William Gawkroger were brought before Judge Baron Rolfe
at the West Riding Assizes at Leeds on a charge of burglary at
Cookridge Hall, which is situated about four miles from Otley
(NR). The house was the seat of John Wormald Esq. and on the
night of 25 October 1840, the housemaid Jane Stewart testified
that, as usual, she had shut all the windows on the ground floor
at about 5 p.m. When she arose the next morning at 7 a.m., she
found, to her consternation, that her bedroom door had been
locked on the outside. She tried another door but that was locked
too. Jane went to the front part of the house and down the main
staircase where she found the front door wide open. She woke
the butler and Mr Wormald, who went through into the living
room and found the windows open, with the shutters broken and
hanging off. Mr Wormald also noticed that the front door had
been opened from the inside. Additionally, he found two drawers
which had been broken into in the library and two seals, some
spirits and a gold pencil case stolen. Upon looking outside, he

found that on the ground near the window there were footprints from at least five men. He showed them to the chief constable Mr Read, who advised him to cover and preserve them. He later compared one of the boots of the accused with these footprints and found that it corresponded exactly, even to the nail on the centre of the heel. He took statements from the servants, one of whom testified that a man named Ibbotson had called at the house the day before the robbery enquiring for Mr Wormald. Ibbotson was arrested the same day at Headingley, as were Griffin and Gawkroger. Ibbotson's house had been searched but although none of the missing items had been found, a comparison of Ibbotson's boots proved that he had been part of the gang of burglars at Cookridge Hall.

A prisoner, John Jackson, had met Ibbotson at York Castle where he had been imprisoned. He told the court that Ibbotson had told him he and some others had committed the robbery. Ibbotson had described the layout of the house and had undoubtedly taken part in the burglary. There was a flurry in court when Ibbotson, at this point, announced that he wanted to change his plea from not guilty to guilty. Even more consternation was heard when he stated that the other two men were innocent of the crime. The judge refused to change his plea and stated that the case should continue. Robert Lawson, a shoemaker of Leeds, told the court that he had been offered a seal by Griffin for 7s. Then some very curious and underhanded police methods were uncovered. After some cross-examination, Lawson admitted that he had been employed by the chief constable, Mr Read, to purchase the seal if it was offered to him. He also admitted that he had been in the employment of Mr Read for some months, and had been asked to get acquainted with suspected people involved, in an attempt to gain their confidence. He admitted that by this method he had betrayed some of his most intimate friends who he had known for some years. The defence, Mr Cottingham, requested the jury to discount Ibbotson's statement that he was guilty. He went through all the points to prove Ibbotson was in fact innocent of the crime. He said that he deplored the methods of entrapment which had been revealed by the Leeds police force in order to gather evidence against the prisoners.

Judge Baron Rolfe summed up the evidence minutely for the jury and they only consulted for some minutes before returning a verdict of guilty against Ibbotson and not guilty against Griffin and Gawkroger, who were then removed from the dock.

Despite being discharged, the innocence of William Gawkroger was brought into question with the next case, when along with two other criminals, Charles Wilson and Edward Townsend, he was charged with another burglary. The second burglary had taken place at the house of Amaziah Empson Esq. of Stavely near Knaresborough (NR) on the 23 December 1840. The butler, Thos Rushby, told the court that the previous night he had left a tray containing items for service next morning in the dining room. He listed these as a large silver sugar basin, a mustard pot, a salt seller, two large spoons, two small forks, one teaspoon, a salt spoon and a mustard spoon. In the morning, he found the front door shut but not locked, and the keys and all the articles that had been on the tray had gone. Two chisels had been put on the tray in their place. The evidence upon comparing the marks that were left on the shutter and the window showed that the marks were indeed made by the chisels. Edward Townsend turned Queen's Evidence and told the court of the burglary in which he had been involved. He said that he had known Gawkroger for some years but had not met Wilson until the night of the burglary. He told the judge that after the robbery, the stolen items had been taken and hidden in Harewood Park, where he had recovered them the next day. He had sold the items to a general dealer called Harris. The jury had no option but to declare all the prisoners guilty and the men were then placed at the bar for sentencing. The judge addressed the prisoners severely as he told them:

You, the prisoners, evidently constituted part, if not the whole, of a regularly organised gang of depredators, by whom the neighbourhood around Leeds had long been infested. It had seldom been my lot in the course of my judicial experience to find burglars more deliberately planned and determinedly executed than those which you have been convicted. Nor have I seen many cases in which the proof of guilt was more conclusive. It is plain that you have led dissolute and abandoned lives and I will take care that for a very long portion of your remaining lives that you should work hard and fare ill.

He then sentenced all of the burglars to fifteen years' transportation. I have been unable to find any records for Gawkroger or Townsend, but Charles Wilson was one of 350 prisoners who sailed for Van Diemen's Land on the *Barrosa* on 27 August 1841, to begin his fifteen-year sentence.

As we have seen, the Assizes magistrates handed out the most extreme sentencing when burglaries were accompanied by violence, and these were worsened when elderly people were attacked. On the night of 6 January 1843, Mr John Bradley (87) of Huntington near York (NR) and his wife Elizabeth (around 70) retired for the night, after ensuring the house was secured. At some point during the night, they woke to find four men in the bedroom. The men wore veils to hide their faces and carried club sticks. Demanding money, one of the men went to Elizabeth's side of the bed and, pinching her nose, pulled a pillow over her face. She could hear two other men dragging her husband out of bed and beating him with sticks outside the bedroom door. One of them cried, 'Hang him out he's not dead yet' and when the pillow was removed from her face, she saw that he was pulled by the hair back into the bedroom. The men were wearing smocks but the one who had attacked Mrs Bradley had a dark shirt and waistcoat underneath the smock. During the attack on her husband, this burglar took off the crepe veil and she saw his face. Two of the men stayed in the bedroom for an hour, threatening the old couple, whilst the other two plundered the house. Finally, the gang informed the couple that they were going downstairs, where they would be having something to eat and would be in the house another two hours. They left the bedroom, threatening them that if either of them moved or cried out they would be killed. Mrs Bradley, once she was sure the men had left, alerted a neighbour and the police. Among other items, they found that the men had taken £200 that had been hidden in a box. As a result of her information, an order was given for hand bills with the men's description on it to be circulated throughout the city. On Monday 1 February, Mrs Bradley was asked to go to York

Courtroom scene.

Castle Prison to identify a prisoner who was thought to be one of the gang. She very quickly identified a man named Wilson Rocket, pointing him out as he came down the castle steps. On Tuesday 21 March, Rocket was brought to the York Assizes before Mr Justice Coltman. Despite having three character witnesses who stated that he was a respectable and honest man, Rocket was found guilty. The following day he was sentenced to transportation for life.

A very courageous attitude of a young woman towards burglars was praised by an Assizes judge in the next case. John May (29) and Henry Ross (27) were brought before the judge at York on Wednesday, 7 December 1859, charged with the burglary of a public house. The Fox and Hounds at Slateworth, near Hepworth (NR) was in a very isolated area. The pub landlord was an old man who ran the pub with the help of his two daughters Ann and Elizabeth. On that evening of the 10 March 1859, the house had been secured by the two girls, who retired to bed where they were sleeping in the same room as their father due to his ill health. The second bedroom was occupied by their brother.

At 1.30 a.m. the following morning, the girls were disturbed by three men entering the room and demanding money. Ann got out of bed and seized a gun, handing it to her father and telling him to use it – but before he was able to, one of the men struck him over the head. She grabbed the gun and beat the nearest man as hard as she could with it; the gun broke in two pieces. Elizabeth was shaken awake by another man, later identified as Ross, who was holding an axe. She recognized the axe as being one which had been left downstairs the previous night. Another man, identified as May, then seized Ann and hit her with a life preserver (a long piece of metal which was weighted at one end). The candles were extinguished and the men demanded money. Ann told the men that they could have all the money in the house but she begged for them to spare their lives. She then handed May a purse containing 8 or 9s. He said, 'If this is all you have you must all die.' The men then grabbed the old man and pushed him out of the room. When Ann was able to relight the candle, she found her brother on the floor outside the bedroom, 'bleeding like a sheep'. The two girls went downstairs to find their father also covered in blood, and the three men ransacking the house. They later noted that a quantity of spirits, tobacco and cash had been taken and that the cellar window had been broken. The men finally left, and the constable was immediately called. A few weeks later, the two girls were asked to look at some prisoners to see if any of them were the men who had committed the burglary. Ann identified May; her sister, Elizabeth, identified Ross. When the two men were brought to the Assizes, the judge told them that they had been found guilty of a more violent crime than had ever been before him previously. Because of this, he sentenced them to death, which was later commuted to twenty years.' transportation each at the mercy of the Queen. They both left England on 30 September 1861, amid 306 other convicts aboard the *Lincelles*, bound for Western Australia.

Chapter Ten

Breach of Promise

During the nineteenth century, it was generally accepted that the only way in which a woman could leave the house of her parents was when she got married. The fear of becoming a spinster was paramount in society, and therefore the emphasis was for young women to marry as soon as they possibly could. Consequently, there was a crime which is not heard of today: breach of promise. It was said that when a man 'promised' to marry a girl, if he reneged on the deal, he would be in 'breach' of his promise and he could be brought into the Assizes court. Some cases were not brought to court and were generally forgotten about. However, when a child was born out of wedlock, a father would take the suitor to court to recover payment for the loss of their daughter's reputation. The cases which did go to court were usually serious enough to be heard before a judge and jury, and an amount of money as compensation would be agreed. Throughout these types of cases the man was always portrayed as the villain of the piece and the girl's family's claims to respectability were heard in every single case.

The *nisi prius* court (the court that heard all legal actions) heard such a case on Saturday, 10 March 1836, when a father sued the accused for the 'loss of his daughter's character'. The charged was brought against a Mr Mills, who was said to have 'debauched the plaintiff's daughter by which her father had been deprived of her services and the comfort of her society'. The girl's father, Mr Whitely, was a confidential clerk in the large establishment of Marsden and Co. of Huddersfield (WR). He had a family of nine children, three of whom were daughters. From 1833 to 1836, it seems that Mr Mills, a local brewer and maltster, was on terms of intimacy with the eldest daughter, Elizabeth, and the acquaintance was recognised as one existing between two parties intending to be married. That intimacy terminated with the birth of a child on 8 September 1836. Shortly before her lying-in, Mills asked Elizabeth to go to a different part of the country to give birth. She refused, preferring to remain near to her family and friends rather than to be confined amongst strangers. Mills complained that the shame of having an illegitimate child could ruin him but she stuck to her guns and he disowned her. For some time afterwards, Mr Whitely cherished the hope that Mills might at last do his duty to his daughter. As a consequence, he delayed from instituting legal proceedings in order to prevent the detail of her shame and that of her family from being publicly discussed. Subsequently, it was not until all hope that Mr Mills would marry his daughter was gone that Mr Whitely was obliged to take the matter to court. Mr Whitely's solicitor told the jury that Mills was a man of substance and had ample means to pay compensation for the breach of promise. He pointed out that Mr Whitely had tried to bring up his children for the last twenty or so years, 'with industry, honesty and respectability' and he asked the jury to consider what damages they would think themselves entitled to for one child being:

> ... ruined by the artifice of a man like the defendant and instead of being an honour and a comfort to her family to be perhaps a burden and reproach for the remained of her life. Beside there were other daughters in the family. They all knew how the misfortune of one sister would be made a calamity to the others. And those sisters who before might have had the best prospects of an honourable marriage might continue in his family and the father thus sustained additional injury.

A woman giving evidence in court. (Courtesy of *Mysteries of Police and Crime*)

Elizabeth Whitely took the stand and stated that she was twenty-five years of age, and that she lived with her father. Her fiancé, Mr Mills, had a house on the same street and he would visit her on a weekly basis. This relationship lasted until the time of her confinement, when his visits became less frequent. During the three years of their acquaintance, Mills had often promised to marry her and, as a result, had been received by her family as 'a gentleman paying his addresses to her'. Elizabeth told the court that, although she had known Mills since 1833, they had not been intimate until Christmas of 1835. The witness, who was described by the reporter as being, 'a beautiful and interesting girl' wept frequently during her lengthy examination, which made it difficult for the jury to catch the evidence distinctly. After an address from Mr Mills, in which he corroborated the facts of the case, the judge, Mr Justice Patterson, summed up and the jury found the case for Miss Whitely proved and damages of 300 guineas were awarded to her.

Another breach of promise case took place at Scarborough (ER) and was brought to the attention of the York Assizes on Friday, 13 July 1860. Miss Sarah Gill had managed a lodging house at Scarborough, one of twelve properties owned by her mother and step father. She had met Thomas Love several years before, and he started paying court to her. Sarah's stepfather, Mr Kelly, when he realised that the couple were serious about each other, asked Love whether he was in a position to keep a wife. He replied that he was perfectly well able to do so, and told her stepfather that he had every intention of marrying her. Love travelled around the country as part of his employment, and he sent several warm and affectionate letters to her from places where he stayed. The defence stated that he did not intend to read out the letters in full but that he would refer to them to indicate the affectionate nature of his client towards Sarah. In some he referred to himself as 'your affectionate Tom', and in others as 'your miserable Tom'. The letters were addressed to 'my sweetest Sarah' and 'my dearest Sarah'. By the end of 1857, relations between the couple had cooled somewhat, which they stated was due to their different religions. Love stated that Gill was Roman Catholic and he was Protestant, and that, to be truly married, one of the other of them should convert to the other's faith. By the summer of 1858, Love went to Scarborough and, once again, the relationship was resumed. He wrote to his 'dearest girl', stating that being without her was like 'tearing away a part of himself'. However, this affection did not last long and the relationship cooled once more, as Sarah continued to be concerned about her religion. Love wrote to her towards the end of 1859, asking for all his letters back and stating that he was prepared to return hers. Gill, however, refused to comply with his request. To her complete shock, in the beginning of 1860, she heard that he had married another woman. Her mother and stepfather came into the court and gave the jury an indication of her distress when she had heard that Love had married, and how ill and depressed she had become as a consequence. Love appeared in court and stated that he had loved Sarah deeply, but there had been no contract between them, and that – if there had been – it would have had to be conditional due to the different faiths. The jury retired for half an hour before awarding damages of £87 to Sarah.

The next case involves a couple who had known each other for about sixteen years, before the defendant, without any reason, married someone else. The case of Sarah Sands versus John George Clapham, both of Leeds (WR), was heard at the York Assizes on Saturday, 9 March 1861. Miss Sand's solicitor was a Mr Blackburn, who told the court that she had been brought up a very respectable young woman who, at the age of thirty-seven, still lived at home with her mother. Her mother was paralyzed and unable to work and so Miss Sands had taken up dressmaking to make ends meet. The defendant, Mr Clapham (35), was a cloth manufacturer who owned the Booth Royd Mill at Batley, near Leeds. The couple met after being introduced by a mutual acquaintance at the local chapel, and, after a short while, he proposed to her and she accepted. Miss Sands told the jury that Mr Clapham was a Methodist preacher, and she had often met him at the Methodist minister's house, where she would help him to write out the week's sermons. Despite the fact that her father had found Mr Clapham not good enough for her, being 'only a manufacturer', he was polite to the young man, who visited his daughter two or three times a week, and had accepted him as her future husband. On being informed that her father would have preferred someone of a higher status, Clapham told her that he would 'never give her up' and that her father's opposition only made him 'more determined to marry her'. In 1855, her health began to suffer and so she went to Ilkley to recuperate. During her stay, she received a letter from Clapham, stating that his thoughts were 'constantly at Ilkley', and ending with, 'a hundred kisses'. She recovered from her illness and returned home, where the relationship continued. Mr Clapham took the stand and told the jury that he admitted, in the presence of others, that 'nothing on earth' should separate them. He stated that he had his portrait taken, which he presented to her in May 1856. He declined to give any reason why he had discontinued the courtship, or why in October of 1860 he had married a Miss Carnie. When asked by Mr Blackburn whether he was aware of the effects his new marriage had on Miss Sands, he stated that he knew that she had been suffering severely from 'depression of the mind and disappointment', and he had heard that she had 'fallen into a decline, not being a very strong woman'. Mr Clapham stated that he had offered a sum of money to Miss Sands in compensation, but she had felt that it was not enough, and she wanted more than he could give. He also pointed out to the jury that he might be a manufacturer, but the machinery in his factory was owned by his father and that he had recently put an advertisement in the newspaper to inform people of that fact. Indeed, he stated that he was not a wealthy man and therefore would be unable to pay a large amount in damages. In fact he ran his business on a very small capital and never had more than £300 in the world. He called his father to the stand, who informed the court that his son owed him somewhere in the region of £650. Mr Blackburn, on behalf of his client, pointed out to the jury that Mr Clapham would be expected to draw £1,000 a year from his manufacturing business.

Mr Temple, who was speaking on behalf of Mr Clapham, told the court that Miss Sands had always had delicate health during the time of her acquaintance with Mr Clapham. He defended his client's actions by stating that he had:

> ... not behaved in any way with any degree of brutality against her; he had not broken off the acquaintance in a manner calculated to insult her: nor did he breathe a syllable against her character or conduct. He was prevented from marrying Miss Sands because it was disagreeable to his parents, and he did not like to contract a marriage of which his mother and father disapproved.

The judge expressed his pity that a man of thirty-five years was not permitted by his parents to carry out a contract of marriage, stating that a crueller case had not come before a jury. He also offered his opinion that he should be 'made to pay to the fullness' of his power. The judge informed the jury that the only issue he had to consider was the amount of damages he would be made to pay following the verdict, and in such a case as this, the jury would be warranted to 'give good substantial damages'. The jury retired to consider their verdict, and when they returned after half an hour they had agreed that the sum of £400 should be paid to Miss Sands.

Much lower was the amount in damages awarded to Phoebe Mason in her case against Mr Furniss. The case was heard in the *nisi prius* court of the York Assizes on 15 March 1862. Phoebe was the daughter of Mrs Mason, a widow and the landlady of the Farfield Inn at Hillfoot, near Sheffield (WR). During the year of 1858, she went to see a friend of hers where she met Mr Furniss. He told her that he had an electro plating business in Sheffield, employing between twenty and thirty workmen. The first time he met her, he asked her to take a walk with him; she would not grant him this request, as she had not met him before. However, upon his second request, she eventually agreed. After this walk, he escorted her home and introduced himself to her mother, declaring that his intentions were honourable. In due course, the couple became engaged and he was received into the family as her accepted suitor. After being engaged for about a year and a half, Mr Furniss asked her mother if he could have her hand in marriage, to which Mrs Mason replied that she felt her daughter was too young to be married. Nevertheless, after a lot of persuasion she agreed. Preparations for the wedding went ahead, with the bride excitedly choosing her wedding dress. Despite the gaiety of the ongoing arrangements, it was at around this time that both Phoebe and her mother had noticed a change in Mr Furniss's manner. It seems that, given the parlance of the time, 'she had given in to him and as a consequence he had ruined her'. Phoebe had confided in her sister and asked her opinion of what she should do when she had not heard from her fiancé for three weeks. Her sister went to see Mr Furniss to ask him what he proposed to do about the fact that he had seduced Phoebe. He assured her that he was an honourable man, and that he would do his duty and marry her 'within the week'.

Following this, a previous employer named Mrs Laycock of Stumperlowe Grange, asked Phoebe to accompany her on holiday. Phoebe agreed and went on the holiday, no doubt picturing the nuptials that would go ahead on her return. She was confounded and devastated to learn that, in her absence, Mr Furniss had married a cousin, a woman with a greater fortune than Phoebe. Her sister showed her the report of his marriage in the local newspaper. At the time he assured her sister that he would marry her 'within the week', he was already making plans to marry his cousin. Grief-stricken and depressed about his cowardly and humiliating rejection, she was horrified to find that she was pregnant with his child. She was just twenty years of age when she gave birth to a baby boy on 20 February. She told the jury that 'thus, in shame' she was compelled to go before the jury and admit her seduction and ask for compensation for the 'loss and injury' she had 'sustained'. The reason for the rejection was made clear when the judge was told that the money which the newly married Mrs Furniss had brought to her husband was 'enough to buy a public house at Crosspool'. The counsel for Phoebe stated:

> Mr Furniss had repeatedly gone to the house of the shamed woman as her engaged fiancé and had been received by them in whom perfect trust and reliance had been placed and succeeded on the assurance that he was about to marry her and as such had accomplished her ruin.

He then called upon the jury to allow the girl such damages as they thought that Mr Furniss could afford to pay to her. Several witnesses were called who all spoke highly of Phoebe and the respectability of her family. The judge stated that it had been clearly proved that a promise had been made and broken and they must give a sum which they felt would compensate for the damage sustained by the conduct of Mr Furniss. The jury agreed and awarded her damages to the sum of £150.

A very cool and calculating character appeared in front of the judge in August 1874. The man, named Houseman, was the eldest son of a large sheep farmer at Hidden Carr, Middlesmoor near Pateley Bridge (NR), and it was whilst he was attending to his father's sheep that he met Miss Verity. Very quickly the couple fell in love, and towards the end of 1873 he promised to marry her; the date was set for the 1 April 1874. Miss Verity's defence commented at this point in the proceedings that it was a very appropriate date, seeing the 'fool' he had made of her. Miss Verity complained that she had spent £30 of her own money in preparation for the wedding a couple of days beforehand, when she had gone to Leeds to do some last minute shopping. She fully expected him to meet her off the train, but he was not there. However, she met him on the way to her mother's house where he was invited for supper. Whilst eating, he coolly told her that he was not going to marry her at the time, as, if he did, there would be a 'lass at Pateley Bridge' who would sue him for 'breach of promise'. He added that his father was against him marrying her 'as she had nowt'.

This calculating young man had gone earlier in the day to Miss Verity's mother's house and whilst her mother had gone out he ransacked her bookcase and took four letters belonging to Miss Verity. One of the letters was from the clergy who had announced the banns and was expecting to marry the couple in a few days time. He casually told her that he had destroyed the letters as 'these would do him harm'. The jury, no doubt aware of his deviousness, awarded damages of £200 to be paid to Miss Verity.

These cases are all about proving the girl's decency, something highly prized by people of this era. However, what we don't see within these cases is the outcome of the matter. Having their private lives discussed within a court of law must have had an impact on the girl and her parents. Would she go on to form other relationships after being so 'ruined' by a man?

Chapter Eleven

Bigamy

Since the Bigamy Act of 1603, this crime was seen as a capital offence. Prior to this, it seems that it was viewed with some sympathy by working class people – who would tolerate such offenses as being preferable to 'living in sin'. Proving that a person was not married was difficult, although the reading out of the banns for three successive Sundays in church services was intended for that purpose. It was generally believed that if a person hadn't heard from their spouse for seven years, they were unofficially presumed dead. However, if they married another person knowing that the spouse was still alive, then that would be deemed as bigamous. The curious thing about these cases of bigamy was the multitude of reasons given to excuse the prisoner of the crime. Nevertheless, it was very difficult to prove and it is probable that many couples got away with it.

One case of bigamy, which was discovered when a man had been recognised, was heard at the Winter Assizes at York in December of 1840. The man, Robert Wilson (27), was charged that on the 2 March 1840, he married Jane Hall at Alne (NR), knowing that his former wife Mary Wilson was still alive. He told the judge and jury that his first marriage had taken place at Nunnington (NR) in 1835. He claimed that due to his wife's infidelity just three years after the couple separated, he then found himself in a 'situation' as a groom at a doctor's house at Alne, where he met Miss Hall. Posing as a widower, he formed a relationship with her. In the beginning of 1840, he asked his master for the hand of his daughter, which was agreed, and the date of the marriage was set. Just a few months into the bigamous marriage, he was recognised by a person from Nunnington, who knew very well that his former wife was still alive. Upon learning of the crime, his former master sent for the police; he was then arrested and brought before the magistrates' court. Despite his protestations of innocence, the jury found him guilty and the magistrate ordered that he be sent to the Assizes to take his trial. The judge told him that there was no reason given to mitigate the crime, and the jury found him guilty and sentenced him to serve one year's imprisonment with hard labour.

Another curious case of bigamy was uncovered at Rotherham (WR) which indicates the attitude that some men had towards their spouse. The jury were told that when a man returned back to the town eight years after he had left, he found that his wife was married to another man. Mr Wilcock told the court that he had been married in 1840, and, after only a few weeks of married life, he deserted his wife and she was forced to enter the Rotherham Workhouse. After some time, he appeared back in the town once more and took her out of the workhouse. Following a short period of time, he again decided to leave her, and enlisted himself in a regiment, which was shortly afterwards sent abroad. When Lucy Wilcock had not heard from her husband for many years, she felt sure that he was dead. When asked by a man named Patrick Foley to marry her, she agreed. Her wayward husband once more returned back to Rotherham, and, finding her married to another man, he protested to the legal authorities and the case was tried at the York Assizes on Saturday, 18 March 1848. The defence put up a good case of mitigation for Mrs Wilcock, stating that she had not heard from her husband for many years and had agreed to marry Patrick Foley in good faith. The lawyer pointed out that it was not an intention to deceive, and in fact the husband had only approached the police authorities when he became aware that Mr Foley was financially quite well off. He questioned that his original plan could have been to blackmail

Rotherham Workhouse.

the couple into keeping silent. When that plan failed, he informed the authorities and the case was sent to the Assizes. The judge and jury agreed that, although she had not meant to deceive, she nevertheless had not made any enquiries to the military authorities as to whether her husband was still alive. As a consequence of this, she was sentenced to a minimum period of three months in the Wakefield House of Correction.

Sometimes the reason for committing bigamy was that the person assumed he could get away with it due to the geographical distance between the first and subsequent marriages. On 7 December 1844 another case was heard by the judge at the York Assizes when an elderly, unnamed man (61) was charged with, on 8 July 1843, marrying Betty Fielding at Heptonstall (WR), 'knowing that his first wife was still alive'. It seems that, two years earlier, he had married Mary Hayes at Heywood in Lancashire and was well aware that she was still alive when he undertook to marry Betty Fielding. During their relationship, he had told Miss Fielding that he was a widower, but after he married her he hinted that there was 'some matter of a stir about Mary Hayes'. No doubt his second 'wife' asked him to explain this, and, when he confessed, she complained to the authorities. When asked by the judge why he had committed the crime, he told him that he thought his first marriage was invalid as during the ceremony 'he had not himself put on the ring'. The judge showed him no sympathy as he ordered him to serve six months in prison with hard labour.

A resourceful and educated man could just about get away with anything if he put his mind to it; no man fitted this description better than Edward Drane Hannebell. He was described as a good looking young fellow who was a coach builder by trade when he was brought to the York Assizes on a charge of bigamy at Hull (ER). In the early months of 1852, he had been working with his father at Ipswich when he met a woman named Ellen Cufley who lived at Manchester but was visiting relatives at Ipswich. When Miss Cufley returned back to Manchester, Hannebell followed and the couple were married at Manchester Cathedral on 6 June 1852.

The couple lived together as man and wife until he left the town to find work. For a short time, he was employed at Bristol and then found work at Hull. In March of 1853, he sent a letter to a prosperous young lady named Miss Crackles, who attended the same church as himself. Apologising for the fact that he had addressed her without being introduced, he asked to meet her, stating that he had never met a woman he wanted to marry until he saw her. He drew her attention to the fact that he also was a dedicated member of the church and stated that it 'was ordained by God that the man should make the first advance'. Despite the fact he wrote that he would leave the matter in the hands of God, Miss Crackles ignored his plea, and it was only a short while before he sent a second letter asking to see her once more. On this occasion, Miss Crackles agreed to meet him and she quickly fell for his charms and a wedding date was set. At the same time as he was petitioning Miss Crackles, he wrote to his wife, who had now returned to Ipswich, stating that he had been unable to find work in Hull and was going to seek his fortune in America where he 'had no doubt of getting a good living'. Instructing his wife to remain at Ipswich, he told her that he would send for her as soon as he had found employment. He ended the letter with terms of great endearment and affection for her. Hannebell and Miss

Crackles were married at Hull on 3 June 1853. But their happiness was short-lived, as the marriage was brought to the attention of the authorities. Hannebell was swiftly arrested and sent to gaol. Whilst in prison he sent two letters; one was to his wife, begging her to get some female to write to her, dating the letter prior to his marriage to Miss Crackles, stating that he was dead. He instructed her that if any enquiries were made, she should tell them that the letter writer had since gone to America. We are not told what the reception of the letter had on his wife, but he begged her to do this for him or he would face transportation for many years. This devious young man then also wrote to the former Miss Crackles, stating that he was confident he would soon be released, as it was all a big mistake and that he looked forward to 'living happily with her for the rest of their lives'. He paid another criminal in Hull gaol to send the letters for him but nevertheless the letters landed in the hands of the authorities. He was brought to the Winter Assizes in December 1853, where the jury took hardly any time at all to find him guilty and the judge sentenced him to six months in prison with hard labour. They expressed their opinion that the case was aggravated 'by being committed under the garb of religion'.

Hull Town Hall. (Chris Drinkall)

Sometimes the reason given for the crime of bigamy was usually that of ignorance that the spouse was still living, but, on 17 March 1860, a less plausible reason was given when Elizabeth Blanco was charged with bigamy at Leeds. She had been married to her first husband at Leeds in June 1855. Elizabeth told the Assizes jury that she had left her first husband due to his ill treatment of her in October 1857. She then went into service to earn a living, and two years later, she was working as a housekeeper to a Mr William Haigh of Scarborough. After only a few months, he proposed to her and she gladly accepted. The judge asked Blanco if she was aware that her first husband was still alive, and she told the jury that because they had been married at a Registry Office, she thought that the marriage was invalid, as 'they had not been married in church'. Neither the judge or jury was impressed with her reasoning, and they sentenced her to one month's imprisonment at the Wakefield House of Correction.

Another curious excuse was proffered in a bigamy case in July 1879 by a man named John Thompson (26), a mill hand at Bradford. On the 7 August, he married Mary Ann Lorimer, knowing that his wife Jane Thompson was still alive. When asked if he had anything to say, he told the jury that at the time he married his first wife, it was in secret and that her father had found out about the ceremony. His father-in-law then told the couple that, because they were both underage, the marriage was illegal. Thompson told the jury that her father had then taken her back to the family home and had forbidden her to have any more to do with him. As a consequence of this, he hadn't seen her for seven years. The judge told him, 'If what you say is true, then it will make considerable difference in the sentencing.' Several witnesses were brought into the court, who attested to the fact that Thompson had lived for many years separately from his first wife, and that, since the marriage, she had continued to live at home with her father. The judge sympathised with Thompson but told him that he should have informed Miss Lorimer that he was already married. He summed up the case for the jury, who returned a guilty verdict but with a request for him to be dealt with leniently due to the circumstances of the case. The judge agreed that there had been mitigating circumstances and sentenced him to just three months in prison.

These were just a few cases that were actually dealt with by the court; many more crimes of bigamy possibly went unreported. There was no easy access to divorce for married couples of that era. However, as we will see in the next chapter, there were far more sinister ways of dealing with an unwanted relative, employers or spouses.

Chapter Twelve

Poisoning

Historically, poisoning was mainly committed by women, although in reality men poisoned their wives and even their children. Without the advantage of forensic science tests like we have today, poisons were tested by tasting, which possibly lead to many miscarriages of justice. Historical records don't always indicate the reason for poisoning, and in the Criminal Chronology there are just a few details about a man named Michael Simpson, who was accused of killing his former employer Thomas Hodgson at Crakehill, near Bedale (NR), in March 1800. It seems that he was accused of giving Hodgson some pills which he had been given by a 'wise man', although he refused to give the name of the man. During this period in history, many people couldn't afford medicine and there were many 'wise' men and women, whose knowledge of medicine was limited, their cures mainly based on folklore. Michael insisted throughout his trial that he was innocent of the charge, but nevertheless he was executed at York on Monday, 17 March 1800. His innocence was proved eighteen months later when another man confessed to the crime.

One young woman, who was convicted of poisoning her husband on 28 March 1835, was brought before the York Assizes accused of murder. Ursula Lofthouse of Kirkby Malzeard, near Ripon (NR), was described as being in a very depressed state

during the trial. The court heard that her husband Robert had been in good health on 6 November 1834, when he called in to see his brother and joined him in eating a meal. The following day, he seemed rather unwell and his wife told him that she had made a cake 'on purpose for thee'. Robert tucked into the cake but after a few mouthfuls declared, 'I don't think I could swallow the piece of cake now in my mouth for all the world.' After vomiting and displaying convulsions, he died a few days later. The surgeon who completed the post-mortem found white arsenic in the stomach of the deceased – his wife was arrested and charged. On the way to York in a gig she told Constable Thomas Thorpe that her husband had 'always been a disagreeable man who had kept her short of money'. At the Assizes, a chemist, Lawrence Harlan, told the jury that she had bought two pennyworth of arsenic from his shop in the village. At first he had refused to supply it, stating that was enough to poison half the village. She replied that it was not for herself and she was buying it on behalf of Mr Thomas Grange, who was a well-respected gentleman of Kirkby Malzeard. Swearing her innocence, she was found to be guilty by a jury who retired for only twenty minutes. The judge showed little sympathy when he condemned her to be hanged on Monday, 6 April 1835. The chaplain of York Castle kept a journal, in which he recorded that he had visited Lofthouse in the morning and evening, and, during that time, she confessed her guilt to him. He also administered the sacraments to herself and two other condemned prisoners on the morning of 6 April, and he wrote that he had attended them all 'at the drop'. The crowds assembled to watch the death of Lofthouse and the two men were said to be enormous.

There were similar crowds at the execution of George Howe (32) of Yarm (NR), who had poisoned his daughter, Eliza Amelia, on 25 January 1849. Howe told the jury that the child had been born at the end of October 1848. His wife died shortly after giving birth on 17 November and Howe went to live with a neighbour, Amelia Wood, who nursed the baby and took care of an older child whilst he went to work. Mrs Wood stated that at first he was a very loving father, but after a short while he was out drinking with companions four or five nights a week. He turned against Wood, asking her, 'Who would want me with two children to care for?' On another occasion, he picked up the baby and squeezed her so tightly that Wood refused to let him handle her any more. On the evening of Sunday 24 January, Howe informed Wood that he had someone coming to pick the child up from Middlesborough. When she questioned why someone should pick a child up so late at night, he became enraged and exclaimed, 'You must have a very bad opinion of me!' Later that night, Wood was feeding the baby some bread and milk in the kitchen, when her nephew called out to her to bring a candle upstairs. She left the baby in her cot in front of the fire whilst she went upstairs. On her return, Howe took the one remaining candle and Wood continued to feed the baby by firelight. After a few moments, the baby vomited a small piece of bread. Upon lighting another candle, Wood looked at the bread and milk and found it to be of a more watery consistency than before. The child's mouth appeared to be blistered and the tongue was swollen. Tasting the bread, she found it burned her tongue and she took it upstairs to her uncle, Mr Bray, and one of his lodgers, a man named Holmes. They also tasted it and, remarking on its acidity, they took the remaining food to the surgeon's house for analysis.

The surgeon, Mr Dale, immediately called the local constable, a Mr Hardcastle, who went to the lodging house and searched Howe's bedroom. The constable found a piece of white paper with some crystals, which he tasted and found to be of a 'nasty' flavour. He then arrested Howe for 'attempting to poison his child'. The child was given some magnesia from the chemist but it continued to deteriorate and died the next morning. After the baby had died, Constable Hardcastle searched Howe's room once more and found a piece of sacking – inside it was a bottle containing more crystals.

Following the discovery of this damning evidence, Howe was arrested for murder of Eliza Amelia and taken to Stockton for his trial. Found guilty, he appeared at York Assizes on 3 March 1849.

A witness told the court that Howe seemed to resent the fact that his child had lived when his wife had died, and had often stated that he wished her dead. Howe denied all the charges against him, but Wood told the court that she had once said to him, 'George you are the most incorrigible liar and, if you speak the truth, it is by accident.' Throughout the trial, Howe was described as being very solemn and dejected and when the sentence of death was passed upon him, he seemed resigned to his fate. On 31 March, he was led to the scaffold in front of St George's field. As was usually the case with public hangings, a large crowd of people had been assembling since the early hours of that morning. Howe appeared to be very pale and, after being pinioned by the guards, he knelt down on the scaffold to earnestly pray for his soul, accompanied by the prison chaplain. After a short prayer, the hood was placed over his head and the bolt was drawn. The Governor's diary duly records his burial, which was 'eight feet from the condemned cell and nearly twelve feet from the passage wall'.

Poisoning cases were often very difficult to prove – and as the next three cases indicate – although it was unquestionable that the victims had been poisoned. Who had actually administered the poison was less easy to confirm. On Thursday, 7 February 1850 at Doncaster (WR), six people sat down to drink tea in a house on Cleveland Street. The inhabitants of the house were Hannah Wood (63), a widow, and her lodgers, who were Mr and Mrs Sketchley and their daughter Anne Denton, Mrs Slater and her son, Joseph. It was later established that the water used for the tea was kept in a pitcher in the corner of the kitchen, which had been drawn from a common tap in the yard. Shortly after drinking the tea, Mrs Wood collapsed and a surgeon, Dr Fenton, was called the following day. He found the woman to be extremely ill and he also exam-

The Governor records the burial of George Howe. (City of York Council Archives and Local History)

ined Mrs Sketchley and Mrs Slater, who were also unwell. Dr Fenton, recognising the seriousness of the case, called in a more experienced surgeon, Mr Morey, who arrived shortly after 5 p.m. Later that night around 8.30 p.m., Mrs Wood's stepson James and his wife arrived, and James found his stepmother to be in a dying state. He stayed with her until she died at around 5.10 a.m. on the Saturday morning. The post-mortem was carried out later that same day and an inquest was held at the Doncaster Guild Hall on Monday, 11 February 1850. Drs Morey, Fenton and Fairbanks told the coroner that they had found that some 'noxious substance had been ingested by the victim'. James Wood told the court that he had not seen his mother for the last three months until last Friday, when he was told that she was very ill and it was suspected that she been poisoned. The chemist George Walker told the jury that he had gone to the house and there he saw Joseph Slater, who told him that about a fortnight ago he had purchased some mercury for Mrs Wood to kill bugs. He told the jury that when he had returned to the house that morning to ask Slater some questions about matters which were puzzling him, Slater gave different answers and 'appeared uneasy and uncomfortable in his mind'. Joseph Slater was then called to give evidence and the room was silent as he took his place. He stated that there was an understanding between himself and Mrs Wood that they were to be married. After being questioned on one or two points, the coroner adjourned the inquest until the following day.

At the resumed inquest, the coroner summed up the events of the previous day for the jurors. The first witness was Mr James Howarth, another chemist and druggist of Doncaster who stated that a fortnight previously, Slater had purchased a quarter of an ounce of arsenic costing 1 *d*, which Slater claimed was to be used to purify some bedsteads. Anne Denton, the daughter of Mrs Sketchley, told the jury that on the Friday she left the house around 9 a.m. and did not return until 4.45 p.m. when called upon by Joseph Slater, who told her that her mother had been taken ill. Soon after she arrived home, her father was taken ill also. She told the jury that it was common knowledge in the house that Slater and Mrs Wood had discussed marriage. The chemist, Mr Walker, took the stand once again and told the coroner that he had received a note from Mr William West, the analytical chemist of Leeds, in which he most distinctly asserted that arsenic acid commonly called white arsenic had been found in the stomach contents. Mrs Sketchley said Slater had told her that he had bought some arsenic and given it to Mrs Wood to clean the beds with. At the time, she had remonstrated with him for giving Mrs Woods the arsenic, explaining to the jurors that, in her opinion, Mrs Wood would often put things down and ten minutes later she had forgotten where she had put them. Mrs Wood had told her that she and Slater were to be married, and she had reason to believe that they had occasionally slept together. The coroner summed up the case for the jury stating that:

> In my opinion the deceased died from poison, but the jury has no satisfactory proof as to who administered the poison. It does not seem that any extraordinary blame can be attached to Joseph Slater. He had acted in a manner which hundreds of other people might have done and it was clear from the evidence of Sketchley and his wife that the deceased was not fully *compos mentis* as to be entrusted with poison.

He suggested that they leave an open verdict which would leave the case quite clear for any ulterior proceedings.

The jury adopted the suggestion of the coroner and brought back a verdict that 'The said Hannah Wood died on the morning of Saturday 9 February from the effects of poison, but when, how, by whom or by what means the same was administered into the stomach of the said Hannah Wood no evidence thereof doth appear to the jurors present.'

But that was not the end of the case. On 22 February 1850, it was announced that another of the lodgers, Mrs Sarah Slater (76), a widow, had also died from poisoning on Thursday 21 February. She was the mother of Joseph Slater, who a reporter said that 'for some time there had lain some suspicion'. After the death of Mrs Wood, Mrs Slater had been removed to the union workhouse and had been attended to by the surgeon, Mr Withers Moore. He told the inquest that he saw her when she was admitted to the hospital and she was very poorly and complained of pains in her body. He asked her if she had taken any poison and she replied that she 'thought that she had not'. However, the next day she became insensible and remained so until her death. Mr Moore stated that he had undertaken a post-mortem and found in the contents of the stomach the presence of some irritant poison. The jury was out for two hours before coming back with a verdict that the deceased had died from poison taken on or about the 9 February, but once again they were unable to state with any accuracy who had administered the poison. Had Joseph Slater got away with two cases of poisoning, his mother and his intended wife? Unfortunately, there is no evidence to prove either but there was little doubt that he acted extremely suspiciously indeed.

The next case is that of the master of Keighley Workhouse (WR). He was an aggressive man who had treated his wife in a very violent manner for most of their married life. When arsenic was found in her body, like with Joseph Slater, rumours went around the town that he might have poisoned her. John Sagar (46) was brought to the Yorkshire Spring Assizes in March of 1858, charged that he 'wilfully murdered his wife, Barbara on 19 December 1857'. The couple had been married for nineteen years and had nine children. Several witnesses gave evidence of the cruel treatment he had inflicted on his wife during her lifetime. The prosecution told the jury that a year previously he had chained her to the bed for hours on end in such a position that she could not sit, stand or lie down. He had also previously locked her in the dead house of the workhouse, and just a month before her death a witness stated that she had seen him seize her by the hair, kick her and drag her by her hair into the parlour of the workhouse quarters.

On Monday 14 December, she had been taken very ill and had been visited by Mary Lister of Keighley. She told the jury that whilst she was in the sick room that Sagar had administered to his wife some tea and gruel. Mrs Sagar had told her in the presence of her husband that she was 'all for dying'. Sagar told her callously that she had 'better make haste about it'. On Wednesday, she was visited by her sister-in-law, Mary Scarborough, who also gave evidence that Sagar had given his wife some medicine whilst she was there, and that Mrs Sagar complained about it being bitter and burning her throat. The workhouse surgeon, a Mr John Milligan, attended her and left some more medicine with Sagar to give to his wife. Sagar's sister, Hannah, told the jury that she had stayed all night with the sick woman and her brother had given her two more doses of medicine and that she was sick both times. She called to her brother about 5 p.m. on the morning of the Friday, when it was clear that Mrs Sagar was dying. Hannah Sagar said that her brother was very distressed shortly before his wife had died and she had never seen him ill treat his wife whilst she was present. The workhouse surgeon gave evidence that he had been called to see the sick woman on Tuesday 15 December and had treated her until her death. He had prescribed some purgative medicine and he stated that he saw no symptoms of arsenic in her system. However, she had been treated for an ulcerated leg prior to becoming ill and he suggested that some external medicines contained arsenic which might perhaps have been absorbed into her system. He gave his opinion that 'she had died from inflammation of the stomach produced spontaneously'. The post-mortem had been undertaken by William Ruddock a surgeon of Keighley, who had taken sections from the stomach and liver which had been sent for analysis to George Morley, a surgeon of Leeds. He gave evidence that the tests proved that there was at least two grains of arsenic in the dead woman's body. He offered his professional opinion that the arsenic had been administered over a period of time and more significantly that it had been given by mouth. Frustratingly, once again, there was no direct evidence that the poison had been administered by Sagar and the jury had no option but to give a verdict of 'not guilty' and he was dismissed.

The next victim, Miss Adamson, was a wealthy elderly lady living at Agbrigg near Wakefield (WR), who had been taken ill around 12 August 1860. A neighbour who often did washing for her, Mary Bateson, testified that, after hearing that she had been taken ill, she went to the house to see if there was anything she required. Bateson went upstairs and found Miss Adamson to be very ill indeed and she gave her a little toast and some water from a pitcher which had been left in the room. Miss Adamson was a Catholic and in the course of his duties she was visited by Father John Brown, who saw the old lady between 2 and 3 p.m. on 12 August. He commented that she told him, 'Oh this fire, this fire that burns within me,' and he told the jury that he had held her hand, which he described as being hot and dry. She called for water and Father Brown witnessed her servant, Emma Stringer, giving her something to drink. He noted that the servant dealt with her mistress in a very affectionate way. On 15 August, the poor woman died and Bateson went to fetch a neighbour, Mrs Link, to help her to lay out the body of the deceased woman. Whilst the two women were engaged in their task, Stringer had told Bateson that Miss Adamson had left her everything in her will. Bateson returned home and had only been in the house an hour when Stringer came to fetch her again, asking her to come with her. Upon entering the deceased woman's house, she found Stringer's mother, her brother and one of her sisters there. Bateson told the court that Stringer's brother was kneeling on the floor writing on a piece of paper. When he finished writing, he asked Bateson if she would sign the paper and she told him that she couldn't read or write and so he asked her to make her mark on the paper. She didn't know what she was signing and no one spoke to her apart from the brother. A little later she saw a cart standing outside the house and saw the brother and the sister leave the house, taking a trunk which was loaded onto the cart.

It seems that there were many rumours spreading about the way in which Miss Adamson had died, and, four months later, an order for the exhumation of the body was given by the Secretary of State, on the suspicion she had been poisoned. It was also announced that Emma Stringer and her two sisters had been arrested for administering the poison. Following the exhumation, an inquest was held before the coroner Mr Thomas Taylor on Monday, 1 October 1860. Father John Brown gave evidence that, a few days after Miss Adamson's death, he had opened his door to find Stringer and her two brothers waiting outside. They told him that Miss Adamson was dead and Stringer, who appeared to be pale and excited, handed him a paper which she said was Miss Adamson's will, asking him for his signature as a witness. Father Brown read the paper which plainly read, 'Miss Adamson hereby makes over to Emma Stringer all her furniture, beds and bedding, plate jewelry, knives and forks etc. As witnessed by our hand.'

Beneath it was a cross and 'Hannah Bateson' written beneath it in a different handwriting. He refused to sign it and asked her if there was a document to the effect that she had left her servant everything in Miss Adamson's own writing. Stringer told him that there was, and the priest replied, 'Then that is all you will need.' If he thought he had seen the last of the three he was wrong. They were back the following day with a cheque for £50, which the bank had refused to cash. He told Stringer that she should have no trouble cashing it, provided she had been authorised to do it. Father Brown then told her that he had heard rumours that she had been removing some of Miss Adamson's property, but Stringer denied this.

The landlord, Mr J. Cartwright, also gave evidence at the inquest that he too had also remonstrated with Stringer for removing items out of Miss Adamson's house in the days following her mistress's death. A surgeon of Wakefield, Mr Nunnery, gave evidence that he was in no doubt that not only was death caused by poison but that it had been administered to her over a long period of time. The jury returned a guilty verdict and Stringer was committed for trial on the charge of the murder of Miss Adamson. However, despite the evidence to the contrary, when the case came to the Assizes on 13 December 1860 it was completely overturned by the judge, Justice Hill, who stated to the jury that he felt the case should not have been brought to the Assizes. He told the jury that he had met with the prosecuting council the previous evening and had gone through the details of the case and that:

> After going carefully through the evidence we thought that we should be best discharging our duty both to the country and the prisoner by not offering any evidence upon the inquisition of the coroner's jury. There will therefore be no evidence and you will acquit the prisoner.

The jury duly found the prisoner not guilty and, after thanking them for her liberation, she left the court a free woman. This astonishing result gave little indication of why the judge should make that decision. As we have seen, Assizes judges clearly saw their will as law and his decision would not be questioned. Perhaps in this case, the judge had to make a decision as to whether hearing the case would be cost effective, even though the evidence seemed to indicate her guilt. Nevertheless, it would seem by these cases that during this period it was easy to get away with murder by poison, unless there was an actual witness to the administration of the poison itself.

Chapter Thirteen

Murder

People murder one another for a variety of reasons; it could be out of jealousy, revenge, hatred or greed. But the differences between murder and manslaughter were that the perpetrator had 'malice aforethought' in carrying out the crime; that is, he or she had a determination that the other should die and made plans accordingly.

In the next case the charge of murder against a policeman uncovered a moral dilemma for the good people of Huddersfield (WR). On Tuesday, 28 April 1840, a person named Alexander M. Smith, a gardener from Stirling in Scotland, went to a market garden in Huddersfield and asked the stallholder the price of a shrub. A row developed and the police were called and Smith was taken to the lock up at the police house owned by PC William Dukes. At about 6 p.m., three police officers went into his cell to search him as he was making some noise in the cell. Dukes was the first officer to enter, and the prisoner pulled out a knife and stabbed him. The two other officers, Dawson and Dalton, attempted to rescue Dukes and both received stab wounds, but Smith finally had the knife knocked out of his hands and was handcuffed. Dukes died about twenty-five minutes later and PC Dawson was removed to the infirmary where it was stated that 'he remained in a very precarious state'. An inquest was held on Wednesday morning at the George Hotel, where PC Dalton gave his statement and the jury returned a verdict of wilful murder. Smith appeared to be quite composed when the coroner asked if he wished to say anything.

'Are you satisfied with what you have gotten [the evidence]?'

'Perfectly,' the coroner replied.

'Why then, let's be doing,' replied the prisoner. He was then placed in a chaise and taken to York Castle.

The following week, many religious females went to the aid of the disconsolate police widow and a resolution was taken to raise £500 for her by subscription. A committee was formed and door-to-door collections were made. So abhorrent was the news of the crime that within only a few hours, £150 was raised as male teams vied with female teams to raise the agreed sum. But everything came to a halt when it was rumoured that Mrs Dukes was in fact married to someone else. She had a husband in London whom she had left to go to Huddersfield with Dukes, who similarly had left a wife and eight children. Whilst in London he was known as William Hart, until he went to Huddersfield where he was then known as William Dukes. These reports astounded the God-fearing matrons of Huddersfield, who at first refused to believe the stories, but upon making enquiries from the widow she agreed that the stories were true. The religious group was in a quandary as to how to proceed, and it was suggested that the money go to the real widow until it was established that she had since died. The children of the murdered policeman were said to be in a London workhouse and it was suggested that they should have it, but others thought it should be given back to the donors. However, some of them were so ashamed that they had been duped that they refused to accept it.

Smith was brought to the crowded courtroom at the York Assizes on Tuesday, 21 July 1840. The first person to give evidence was John Dalton, the police officer from Huddersfield, who described how he saw the prisoner stab Dukes in the groin. When he was questioned about Smith's state of mind he told the court that he was in a state of excitement, but when travelling to York with him they had a normal conversation. A surgeon who was present when he was admitted to York Castle Prison asked him ,'My man were you in liquor at the time?' to which he replied,

'No I never was in liquor in my life, but liquor has been in me many a time.' The defence of the prisoner was that he had been subject to epileptic fits for most of his life, resulting in having a 'weak intellect and depraved moral feelings'. Therefore, he claimed that the prisoner was not capable of knowing right from wrong. A witness, Thomas Noble of Elland, near Huddersfield, stated that Smith had lived with him for six months and during that time had several epileptic fits. Two more surgeons, one from Elland, who had known the prisoner, and another surgeon from York Castle, both attested that Smith was insane. The judge summed up the case and after an absence of one hour and twenty minutes they returned with a verdict of 'not guilty on the grounds of insanity'. Smith was therefore sentenced to be detained until Her Majesty's pleasure was known.

As we have seen, many murderers are villains of a truly cruel and vicious nature, who coldly premeditated the death of another. On the night of 18 June 1841, between 11 p.m. and midnight, a woman named Mrs Mary Snow heard groaning coming from the next doors public house at Knaresborough (NR). From her yard, she could see into the window of the pub. She witnessed three men beating someone who lay on the ground. The owner of the pub was a man called Joseph Cocker (56) and lived alone. Mrs Snow ran to the front door of the pub and tried the door but it was locked. Returning back to her home, she woke her husband – demanding he call the police. While he was dressing, she once again ran out into the yard and looked through the window. The men were still inside, and Cocker was leaning against the chimney breast, with blood running from wounds on his head. Her husband joined her in the yard, and, as they both looked through the window, they saw Cocker slumped to the ground and one of the three men rifled through his pockets; all three men then escaped out of the house. PC Vickerman arrived shortly afterwards. Neighbours that had been awakened by Mrs Snow's shouts were now standing in the yard. Vickerman said that he was going into the public house, and some of them agreed to go with him.

They found Cocker was still alive, but barely so; his body was surrounded by a pool of blood. A poker was seen lying partly across his legs and partly on a brass fender in front of the fire.

Blood was spattered all around the floor, the walls and over a long bench. Within minutes of entering the house, Cocker was now found to be dead. Mrs Snow and her husband gave such an accurate description of all three of the men that within the hour they were found in different parts of the town. So quickly had the men been taken into custody that when they arrived at the police station all of them still had bloody evidence on their body and clothes. The men were identified as John Burlinson (24), Charles Gill (19), and Henry Nuttall (22).

The following morning, having had time to think, Nuttall made a confession to PC Vickerman. He told him that on the previous night he had gone to the pub around 10 p.m. and had consumed two or three pints of ale. He then went into the yard to the toilets. When he returned, he found Cocker on the floor and Gill and Burlinson stood over him. In a separate interview, Gill told Vickerman that he and Burlinson had gone into the pub about 10.30 p.m. and had several glasses of ale, until about midnight when Cocker told them he was locking up and refused to sell them any more beer. He said that Burlinson, standing by Cocker, wordlessly drew something out of his pocket, before hitting the old man over the head with it. The man fell to his knees and cried, 'Oh lads don't murder me.'

At the inquest held on the body of Cocker, Gill was put on the stand and he told the coroner that he had made a statement to Vickerman that Burlinson and Nuttall had gone to the pub the previous night, intending to kill the old man. Whilst doing so, they were disturbed by another man, William Inchboard, coming into the pub. He said that he was unaware of the intention to murder, but Burlinson refuted this statement by saying that Gill knew very well that they intended killing and robbing Cocker. The weapon had been a long hammer, the property of Nuttall, which after the murder had been thrown into the river. Nuttall told the jury that Gill had struck the man four or five times whilst he lay propped up against the fireplace. William Inchboard, a tallow chandler, told the jury that Nuttall had been in his employ until he was arrested. After the murder, he had found that part of an adze, which had been in his shop, had disappeared. He described going into the pub on the night before the murder and identified Burlinson and

Gill as leaving the pub before him. The three men were found guilty and sent to take their trial at the York Assizes on Monday, 19 July 1841. Nuttall's defence claimed that he was innocent of all charges – as he had not planned the murder, nor expected it. When returning from the yard, the old man had already been attacked and Nuttall denied taking any further part in the murder. Burlinson and Gill pleaded guilty to manslaughter alone. After a consultation of only fifteen minutes, the jury found all three men guilty. The judge put on the black cap and looked directly at all three men, who appeared shocked by the verdict. He told them:

> You have been convicted on the clearest evidence of a foul and cruel murder on the unfortunate deceased. There is no hope for you in this world and I exhort you to prepare for that future state in which you must enter. A most painful duty remains for me to pronounce upon you the sentence of death.

The triple execution was set for noon on Saturday, 7 August 1841. All three men were attended by the chaplain of York Castle, Revd W. Flower, and Revd J. Rattenbury, a Wesleyan minister, during their stay in the condemned cell. The two ministers also attended the three men on the scaffold. It was reported that all the men remained penitent and prepared themselves earnestly to meet their maker. They walked confidently across the castle yard from the condemn cell to an anteroom of the scaffold, where they were pinioned and allowed to say their last prayers. Gill was placed in the middle with his two comrades on either side of him. It was reported that Burlinson and Gill did not die straight away and continued to struggle for a short while. The Governor recorded that all three men were buried in one grave near to 'a circular passage in a grave nine feet deep'.

In the conclusion of some cases, the condemned may have been given a Queen's pardon. George Blackburn was a small farmer who supplied milk to the people of Barnsley (WR). He lived at Elmhurst Farm near Bank Top, about a mile from the town centre, and every Monday he usually left the house between 11 and 12 a.m. to collect the money from his customers. On 5 October 1840 he was returning home about 4.45 p.m. and had

The prison chaplain's entry in his diary, regarding the execution of Gill, Burlinson and Nuttall. (City of York Council Archives and Local History)

just turned into the narrow lane leading to his farm, where he was seen by his servant, Emma Fretwell. The lane was opposite the barracks and the sentry on duty also saw him heading for home.

Fretwell had previously seen four men behind a wall of the lane and had shouted to them, asking, 'What are you chaps doing there?' Receiving no reply, she returned back to her duties in the kitchen. She saw Blackburn also ask the men what they were doing and without a warning, saw one of them leap onto the wall and fling a large stone at Blackburn's head. Fretwell screamed and ran to tell her mistress what was happening. By the time the servant reached the injured man's side, the men were running up the lane being chased by Mrs Blackburn shouting, 'Murder!'

Four soldiers came and helped carry the injured man into the farmhouse. A doctor was called, and he noted that the injured man was now bleeding from the mouth and nose; within a few hours he was dead. Two of the three men were identified by Fretwell and Mrs Blackburn as being John Mitchell (17) and George Robinson (23). The police conducted enquiries and, as a result, two more men named John Cherry (24) and William Fox (23) were also arrested.

An inquest was held on the body of George Blackburn on Friday 15 October and the jury returned a verdict that the four men were guilty, and sent them to take their trial at York. The men were brought before the judge on 20 March 1841, where Mitchell was charged with murder for actually throwing the stone, Fox with aiding and abetting and Cherry and Robinson as accessories before and after the fact. There must have been little evidence against Cherry and Robinson; as soon as the trial started, the defence and his Lordship agreed that there wasn't enough to convict them and the two men were dismissed. The constable, Thomas Jennings Carnelly, showed the court the huge stone which had been used in the murder. The post-mortem showed that Blackburn's skull had been so extensively fractured on the right side that it had severed an artery. After hearing all the evidence, the judge summed up for the jury, concluding that the evidence against Mitchell was very strong, but against Fox, was rather weak. The jury returned after only half an hour, finding Mitchell guilty, but Fox not guilty. Fox was ordered to stand down and the judge put on the black cap. Before he could ask Mitchell whether there was anything he wanted to say as to why a sentence of death should not be passed on him, there was such a tremendous storm of hail and rain that the proceedings were forced to be suspended for a few minutes until it abated. When the question was put again to the prisoner, he was unable to reply. Interpreting this as consent, the judge stated:

John Mitchell, it is my painful duty at the close of this investigation to pronounce that sentence which the law has imposed on offences such as that for which you have been arraigned. I regret, indeed, that one so young should have placed himself in such a situation as to stand convicted not only of the offence of murder, but, I must add, of murder under such circumstances of great atrocity. Although some of your companions have for the present escaped the vigilance of the law, depend upon it they can never, while they live, be in a state of security against detection and such punishment as shortly awaits you. I can only enjoin you to enjoy the few days that remain to spend in penitence and to reconcile yourself to that Almighty Judge in whose presence you must shortly appear.

Mitchell appeared to be unmoved whilst the judge read out the death sentence and with a stern face he left the dock. The *Northern Star* published a confession written by Mitchell from 'the condemned cell', dated 22 March 1841, where he named Robinson as being the man who threw the coping stone. He also claimed that he had not gone out with the intention of murdering anyone, and had just followed the other three men concerned in the case. This was followed by a three-week series giving an account of his life, where he claimed that he was in a gang which included Cherry, Robinson and Fox and stated that altogether they had committed over a thousand robberies. Then on 1 May, a letter was written by Fergus O'Connor, a celebrated Chartist reformer who was a prisoner in the castle, written on behalf of the Governor, requesting that no more be published on account that it may frustrate the ends of justice. O'Connor included in the letter the sentence 'subsequent to his pardon', which indicates that, because of his confession, Mitchell was granted a pardon and set free.

The Assizes jury heard a case of murder in January 1844 where a man was so provoked that he shot his own father. Joseph Dobson was a weaver who lived at Mount Tabor near Halifax (WR). His mother had died when he was just five years old, leaving him and two other children to be brought up by their father. From an early age, his father beat him and his siblings unmercifully. Dobson started work as soon as he could, but his father insisted that he must hand over his wages, whilst he himself lived in idleness. On one occasion, having eaten no more than watery porridge for days, Dobson took his wages, intent on buying some meat, but when he arrived home his father beat him cruelly with a rolling pin, taking the money and locking him in the house. The following day, he went to Wakefield (WR) where he found work and he lived there for almost three years. Meanwhile, neighbours who had heard the severe beating inflicted on Dobson had not seen him leaving the house since; they were convinced that the senior Dobson had killed his son. They reported the matter to the police who investigated and eventually found Dobson working at Wakefield. The relations between the father and son continued to deteriorate, and, eventually, Dobson joined the army. After a short while, he began to receive letter after letter from his father, encouraging him to leave the army and return home. Dobson did so, and his father used this knowledge to terrorize him into doing his bidding, threatening to report him to the army authorities. Dobson eventually got married and had two children. However, it was not long before his wife was complaining about him being forced to surrender part of his wages to his father every week.

Dobson senior retaliated by threatening to murder her in the presence of the young man.

On 4 July 1843, Dobson and his father began quarrelling again, and the old man once more threatened to kill his wife, stating that he had bought a razor with which to do the deed. Dobson (junior) told his wife, 'Don't worry, it will be the last thing that he does if I can find powder and shot in Halifax.' He borrowed a gun from a neighbour and then went to a shop in Halifax, owned by Hannah Longbottom, where he bought an ounce of gunpowder, some caps and shot. Returning back to his father's house at 3 p.m., he asked him, 'Are you going to do what you said? If you are, I will take the first chance.' His father responded, 'Shoot me, shoot me!' Dobson raised the gun and shot at his father but the gun misfired and he calmly re-filled the gun with powder and shot him in the chest. Before any action could be taken, Dobson went on the run and was not found until October, in Huddersfield. He was returned to Halifax, where he was found guilty and sent to York Assizes for trial in December 1843. The judge, on hearing that Dobson had no defence due to his poverty, appointed one of the solicitors to defend him on the morning of the trial. His defence gave an outline of the terrible treatment of the old man towards his son. He tried to maintain that, due to the provocation suffered by the prisoner, that the charge should be reduced to that of manslaughter, but the jury took just fifteen minutes to find him guilty. The judge asked him if he could say anything in his own defence as to why he should not be sentenced. Dobson replied that, although he had committed the murder and was clearly guilty, his father's cruelty had triggered the act. He stated that his father was also responsible for the death of his mother, three brothers and a sister who had all died as a result of his cruelty towards them. The judge stated that he could not see any grounds for the jury to come to any other conclusion than that they had given, and putting on the black cap sentenced Dobson to death. It was reported that the prisoner's demeanour throughout the trial was 'very composed', and that after receiving the sentence, he seemed 'to resign himself to his fate'. The Governor of York Castle Prison recorded on 8 January that he had allowed Dobson to have a candle in his cell, 'in order that he may have more time to read and pray'. On the 20 January, the day of Dobson's execution, the Governor recorded that despite his composure he was:

> ... only penitent for the last ten days when he finally owned his sentence as just. His body was buried close to the wall under the condemned cell window this evening at 4 p.m. in company with Mr Gray the Under Sheriff and myself.

The chaplain also recorded in his journal that he had accompanied Dobson 'at the drop' and that he appeared to have truly repented of all his sins and that he had a 'firm faith in God's love', for whom he looked to for 'pardon, peace and forgiveness'.

We know that a defence lawyer can be appointed in cases of poverty, such as Dobson's, but in the subsequent case, there were two prisoners who had no defence to speak on their behalf.

William Kendrew (22) was charged with the murder of William Inchbold at Aldborough (NR) in September 1844. The crime was committed as retaliation for Inchbold having threatened Kendrew with having him transported for poaching. His brother John (24) was charged with 'feloniously harbouring and maintaining him well knowing him to be guilty'. Inchbold was a retired merchant and on Saturday, 28 September 1844, he had followed his usual custom of attending Boroughbridge market. At about 6 p.m., he

The chaplain's account of the execution of Joseph Dobson. (City of York Council Archives and Local History)

left the Malt Shovel Inn with the intention of walking home. Although he had some ale, he was described as being 'well and sober'. He had just passed a cottage known as Clay's Cottage when Kendrew caught up with him, and without a word being exchanged, shot him in two places in the back and the top of his left arm.

Inchbold died of his wounds on Monday night at 11 p.m. It seems that Kendrew had gone into a shop on the Friday night, owned by a man named Buckle in Boroughbridge, and bought powder, shot and caps. He was seen, by several people, on the evening of the murder on the same road. At 5.30 p.m., he was spotted by a 'little girl' named Mary Yates, acting very suspiciously. When another man approached, Kendrew hid in a goit until he had gone past, but when he emerged from the goit, he openly carried the gun across his shoulders. When Mary Yates gave evidence in court, stating that he was in front of some white gates, Kendrew said to her, 'Thou lies, it was 100 yards past the gate,' thereby incriminating himself. At 7.30 p.m. on the night of the murder, Kendrew left Aldborough with his brother John and they went to Newcastle where they were finally apprehended in a public house in Pilgrim Street by PC Hutchinson.

William and John Kendrew were brought to the York Assizes on 10 December 1844, where incredibly there were three prosecutors but no defence. The prosecution's witness statements went on until 5.45 p.m. on the first day of the trial, but the prisoners offered no statement or witnesses for their defence. The judge took two hours the following day to sum up the case for the jury, who retired to consider their verdict. They found William Kendrew guilty of the murder, but his brother John they found not guilty of 'succouring and comforting him'. The judge placed on his head the black cap stating to the prisoner:

William Kendrew you have been convicted after a long and patient trial upon evidence that has not only satisfied me but what is more important has satisfied the jury... And you have done it under no heat of blood... I cannot but believe now that you had pre-determined this matter over many hours, I may even say days. You dogged his steps and watched him in perfect unconsciousness himself of any danger awaiting him and that as he was going home to his wife you deprived him of his existence. And you have done this with perfect deliberation.

He then sentenced him to death. Kendrew, displaying the same bored expression he had shown throughout the trial, replied, 'Thank you, if that be all.' However, he must have changed his mind by the time he had been in York Prison a while. The Governor, Mr Noble, wrote in his diary two days before his execution that, 'William Kendrew acknowledged the justice of his sentence and seemed to be very penitent.' He was publicly hanged on Saturday, 28 December 1844 at York Castle in front of a very large crowd. He was buried 'under the wall of the condemned cell on the east side of the projection of the wall at 4 p.m.', in the presence of the Under Sheriff and Mr Noble.

Like Kendrew during his trial, many criminals showed no remorse for their actions. One of the least repentant was involved in the following case. On the morning of Thursday, 11 January 1858, William Shackleton, who lived at Commons Farm, Wadsworth Moor near Halifax (WR), looked out of his window at 8 a.m. and saw what he at first thought was a heap of manure. It was not until the afternoon before he went to examine it, and, to his horror, found that it was the body of a man lying on his left side, covered with blood. He ran to his neighbour, William Greenwood and they took the body to the Hare and Hounds, a nearby public house. As they were lifting the body up, Greenwood picked up a knife which had been lying at the side of the man, but Shackleton told him to put it down until the constable had seen it. He also noted a large stone lying near to the head of the dead man, which he described it as a coping stone taken from a nearby wall. The body was identified the next day as being that of a local farmer, Bethel Parkinson. Inspector John Nicholson from Hebden Bridge went to the murder scene and noted that the large stone found at the scene of the crime had human hairs on it and there was also a broken blade near the body. His wife, Mary Parkinson, told the police that she was a weaver at a nearby mill and had risen early on Wednesday 13 January, leaving her husband in bed. She put two and a half gold sovereigns and some silver coins on the table beside the bed before she went to work. Parkinson was next seen at a beer house known as Raggilds Inn at 8 p.m. on the same night, in company with Joseph Shepherd (22). The two men stayed in the pub drinking together until about 2 a.m. Shepherd was next seen by a cabman, one William Birch, who had known him for about two years. He asked him to take him up into the town but he asked the cabman to go the back way as he 'did not want to be seen'. The cabman drove him to his lodgings, where he got down from the cab and paid him the four pence fare. On the evening of Saturday 16 January, Shepherd was arrested by Thomas Spiers, Superintendent of the West Riding police at the Halifax police station, on suspicion of the murder of Bethel Parkinson. He was tried at Halifax Magistrates' Court and found guilty, and ordered to go for trial at the York Assizes. He was brought into the courthouse at York on Monday, 11 March 1858, where witnesses spoke about the sightings of the two men together, and then later, Shepherd on his own. The jury retired and after fifty minutes returned with a verdict of guilty. Shepherd left the dock and was led away – his face as impassive as it had been throughout the trial. During the time of his incarceration at York, whilst waiting to be hanged, Shepherd showed little remorse or concern for the desperate plight in which he found himself. On the eve of his execution, Shepherd was visited by the prison chaplain Revd J. Parkes, who asked if he wanted him to pray for him. The prisoner laughed out loud, and when he remonstrated that there would be no rest in the next world, Shepherd replied that he had 'better get some rest whilst he could', and promptly lay down on

Halifax Magistrates Court. (Courtesy of Sue Trickey)

the bed. A few hours later, he was visited by the Governor of the prison, Mr Noble, who told Shepherd that if he didn't repent of his sins he would surely go to hell. Shepherd laughed and said, 'At least I will be warm.' On Saturday 3 April at half past eleven, Mr William Grey Esq., the Under Sheriff for the county, the Governor and Deputy Governor, Mr Green and the Revd Parkes, arrived at the condemned cell to escort Shepherd to the scaffold. It had been reported that the building of the scaffold had started at 4 a.m. in the morning, and, as early as an hour later, people were already congregating to see the execution. The executioner was once again Askern from Rotherham, who had been at the prison since the previous night. On the scaffold, Shepherd knelt down in prayer and the nearest he came to a confession was to ask the Lord 'to have mercy' on his soul. He then jumped up quickly to be pinioned by his arms and legs. The noose was put over his neck and the bolt drawn; the crowd noted that he had struggled for a while before becoming still. Such was his notoriety that he was hanged in front of one of the largest crowds seen at York, which was estimated to be from 10,000 to 20,000 strong. His death was

Bibliography

Primary Source Material

Calendar of Felons, 8th March 1785–1799, Ref. No.Y365
Calendar of Felons, 8th March 1800 –1810, Ref. No.Y365
Calendar of Felons, 8th March 1820–1842, Ref. No.Y365
Calendar of Felons, 8th March 1842–1843, Ref. No.Y365
Governor's Journal, 1843, Volume 1, Ref. No.Y365
Chaplains Book York Castle, 1833 Ref. No.Y365

All the above were reproduced courtesy of City of York Libraries, Archives and Local History Department.

Armley Goal Register 1851–3, Ref. No. C187/3/2/1
Calendar of Prisoners Tried at the Spring Quarter Sessions at the Court House Wakefield Ref. No. QS7/31

All the above are courtesy of Wakefield Archives.

Secondary Source Material

Books:

Burdekin, C.L, *Criminal Chronology of York Castle* (1867), Courtesy of Driffield and Wolds Genealogy, 2004 witnessed by his father, mother and his wife. Also in the crowd of people were the father and the widow of Bethel Parkinson. As was usual, the body, after being suspended for an hour, was cut down and the remains buried within the precincts of the prison.

So ended the lives of some of the worst Yorkshire villains. The fact that they displayed true penitence at the end does not make up for the fact that they showed no mercy towards their victims. It is said that the cells below the York Castle Prison are haunted, and, the cases listed in this book provide sufficient evidence for speculation. Thankfully, the majority of Yorkshire people today remain law abiding and respectable citizens, and have a reputation for hospitality and friendliness. The county remains one of the most beautiful in the UK, and is visited by thousands of tourists throughout the summer months.

Other titles published by The History Press

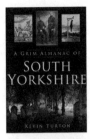

A Grim Almanac of South Yorkshire

KEVIN TURTON

A Grim Almanac of South Yorkshire is a collection of stories from the county's past; some bizarre, some fascinating, some macabre, but all equally absorbing. Revealed here are the dark corners of the county, where witches, body snatchers, highwaymen and murderers, in whatever guise, have stalked.

978 0 7524 5678 2

Murder & Crime: Sheffield

MARGARET DRINKALL

The grim and bloody events in this book, many of which have not been written about for more than a century, reveal the dark heart of Victorian Yorkshire. Some of these gruesome tales would not look out of place in a work of fiction, and will certainly interest those fascinated by Sheffield's shady past.

978 0 7424 5568 6

Sheffield Crimes: A Gruesome Selection of Victorian Cases

MARGARET DRINKALL

This volume collects together the most shocking criminal cases from Sheffield's Victorian newspapers. Richly illustrated with photographs from private collections and from the local archives, *Sheffield Crimes* will fascinate residents, visitors and historians alike.

978 0 7524 5820 5

Murder & Crime: Harrogate & District

JAMES ROGERS

Drawing on a wide selection of sources, this collection of grisly tales explores the shadier side of Harrogate's past. *Murder & Crime: Harrogate & District* will be sure to captivate and horrify everyone interested in the criminal history of this part of North Yorkshire.

978 0 7524 5622 5

Visit our website and discover thousands of other History Press books.

www.thehistorypress.co.uk

Newspapers:

Northern Star and Leeds General Adviser
Rotherham Advertiser
Sheffield and Rotherham Independent

Photographs of York Castle reproduced courtesy of York Museum Trust (York Castle Museum).

First published 2011

The History Press
The Mill, Brimscombe Port
Stroud, Gloucestershire, GL5 2QG
www.thehistorypress.co.uk

British Library Cataloguing in Publication Data.
A catalogue record for this book is available from the British Library.

ISBN 978 0 7524 6002 4

Typesetting and origination by The History Press
Printed in Great Britain
Manufacturing managed by Jellyfish Print Solutions Ltd

YORKSHIRE VILLAINS

ROGUES, RASCALS AND REPROBATES

MARGARET DRINKALL